WOODEN-BODIED VEHICLES

Buying, Building, Restoring and Maintaining

WOODEN-BODIED VEHICLES

Buying, Building, Restoring and Maintaining

COLIN PECK

THE CROWOOD PRESS

First published in 2013 by
The Crowood Press Ltd
Ramsbury, Marlborough
Wiltshire SN8 2HR

www.crowood.com

British Library Cataloguing-in-Publication Data
A catalogue record for this book is available from the British Library.

ISBN 978 1 84797 491 4

Acknowledgements
In compiling this book I have drawn on the immense experience, ingenuity and resources of
numerous vehicle bodywork restorers and builders, both professional and amateurs, from
around the world: without their help this book would just not have been possible. So, it is
dedicated in part to all those people who have been involved in this immense project, and also
to all those future restorers and builders who may draw inspiration from reading its content.

   Due to the book's sheer size and depth it is not possible to attribute specific images
to individuals, as there have been so very many. In addition I would like to offer a sincere
and special vote of thanks, in no particular order, to Peter and Sandie Bayliss of Clanfield
Coachbuilding (UK); Warren Kennedy and Gary Tuffnell at Classic Restorations (UK); Cumbria
Classic Coaches (UK); Peter Delicata at Delicata Coachbuilders (UK); Sebastian Marshall of Historic
Vehicle Restorations (UK); Steve Foreman at Forwoodies (UK); Lyle Meikle and Chris Hinks at
Wicked Coatings (UK); Ron Heiden of Heiden's Woodworking (USA); Glenn Redding of Redding
Woodworks (USA); Eric Johnson at Treehouse Woods (USA); Rick Mack at Rick Mack.com (USA);
Doug and Suzy Carr at Wood N'Carr (USA); Chip Kussmaul at Cincinnati Woodworks (USA); and
Evan Westlake at Grain-It Technologies (USA).

   I would also like to offer a vote of thanks for the personal involvement of Tim Baker, Chris
Bewick, Geoff Boyd, Paul Brook, Ian Brown, Trevor Burrows, Joe Cocuzza, David Fetherston, Alan
Flowers, Charles Furman, Brian Glass, Jim Grace, Frank Healey, Peter van den Heuvel, Paul James,
James McIntyre, Derek McLeish, Bill Munro, Norman Reynolds, Phil Robertson, Peter Russell,
Graeme Rust, Richard Smith, Bryan Smothers, Ian Strange, Mike Walker and Jeff Yeagle.

Typeset by Jean Cussons Typesetting, Diss, Norfolk

Printed and bound in Malaysia by Times Offset (M) Sdn Bhd.

CONTENTS

Introduction

Wood was the material of choice for a large number of vehicle bodies from the dawn of the automobile until well into the 1950s. As a carryover from the era of the horse and cart, wood could be cut and shaped with hand tools, was relatively easy to craft into intricate shapes and – perhaps best of all – it was in plentiful supply.

The art of coachbuilding – a term derived from the horse-drawn coach era – saw wood framing used on everything from van, truck and bus bodies through to a wide variety of automobile bodies, ranging from the cheapest family sedans and open roadsters to the most expensive hand-built limousines and convertibles. In the early days of motoring most vehicle manufacturers only supplied the rolling chassis, leaving the customer to engage a coachbuilder to skilfully craft bodywork to their own specific design and requirements.

In fact, before World War II virtually all ultra-luxury vehicles were sold as chassis only. For instance, when Duesenberg introduced its Model J, it was offered as a chassis-only option for $8,500. Other examples include the Bugatti Type 57, Cadillac V-16 and all Rolls-Royces produced before World War II. Delahaye had no in-house coachworks, so all its chassis were bodied by independents, which created some of their most attractive designs on the Type 135.

Sleek metal skins were formed over hardwood frames at virtually all of the specialist marques.

Wood framing was the material of choice for vehicle bodywork until well into the 1950s.

The Austin A135 Princess was built using traditional aluminium panelling over ash framing at the Kingsbury, London, works of Vanden Plas. (Courtesy Vanden Plas Owners Club)

Austin also contracted Papworth Industries in Cambridgeshire to build 500 wooden-bodied shooting brakes in 1947 on its 'Sixteen' chassis.

In general, coachbuilding skills were so specialized that most chassis manufacturers procured contracts with favoured coachbuilders to build bodies for their chassis to ensure that quality standards were maintained. While most vehicle manufacturers eventually brought the coachbuilding side of the business in house, the relative ease with which wood could be cut, shaped and formed meant that wood-framing techniques enabled coachbuilders to create a number of stylish and exotic body styles that would have been difficult, if not prohibitively expensive and virtually impossible to produce in small quantities using a metal sub-structure.

Convertibles, limousines and even station wagons (US) or shooting brakes/estate cars (UK) were usually sold in small numbers, and so were often farmed out to specialized coachbuilders for their bodywork.

Coachbuilding was even more diverse at the heavier end of the market where van, truck and bus bodies were usually custom built to meet specific customer and operator requirements. While open truck bodies were often simple, if not crude in design and construction, those built for the bus and coach market often mimicked the styles and aerodynamics of some of the most stylish cars of the day. Yet underneath, they often used the same wooden structure and employed the same joints and the same construction methods as used on truck bodies.

However, while wood proved popular with coachbuilders, wood preservatives were in their infancy, and wooden

bodywork often cracked under load and fell apart, rotted out, or was attacked by wood-munching bugs within a matter of years. While it was common practice

for buses, trucks and luxury cars to have their bodywork replaced, often with a more modern style, after a decade or so of hard use most lightweight vans and

The Foden FE range featured one of the most stylish truck cabs ever offered on a British-built truck.

Trolleybuses began replacing tramcars in the UK from the 1930s onwards, and their sleek modern designs were constructed around a traditional wooden framework.

One of the most notable wooden-bodied vehicles of the era was the vehicle we now generically refer to as the 'woodie'.

family sedans usually ended up on the junk pile once their bodywork started to lose its structural integrity.

One of the most notable wooden-bodied vehicles of the era was the vehicle we now generically refer to as the 'woodie'. While examples were built in many countries of the world, they were most popular in North America and the UK. The overall design and functionality was similar, but they evolved to fulfil totally different market needs.

However, their construction came to an end, almost universally, in the early 1950s as manufacturers switched to building steel-bodied wagons, which were cheaper to make and required none of the maintenance associated with wooden bodies. Also, with the increasing use of unitary bodies it was no long possible to attach structural wood framing.

Curiously, there was one woodie

that was actually launched as wooden-framed coachbuilt cars were being phased out, and that was the British-built Morris Minor Traveller. Launched in 1953, it remained in production until

1971. Wood was, however, used in the framing of specialist car, van, truck and bus bodies well into the 1960s, and in some cases even in the framing of truck cabs.

The wooden-bodied station wagon was developed in the USA from an early form of taxicab, known as the 'depot hack'.

The aim of this book is to serve as an inspiration to anybody who is contemplating the purchase, restoration or even the building of a wooden-framed vehicle, and hopefully to guide them round some of the common problems and pitfalls associated with such vehicles. At the same time it sets out to highlight some of the techniques required to end up with a wooden wonder of which they can be justifiably proud.

Unlike other books, which have focused on high levels of technical data or have drawn on the knowledge and experience gained by one individual working on a single type of vehicle, this book aims to cover as many body types and as many restoration and building techniques as possible to provide the reader with the widest possible spread of possible options and solutions.

There is no way that one single book can be the definitive guide to all coach-building requirements, techniques and vehicle restoration processes, but it should go some way to steering the would-be restorer down the right path. Like many things in life, there are usually multiple possible routes, options and solutions, and this is what this book aims to provide.

In researching the content of this book I found that as fast as one person would say that something could only be done one way, then along would come another individual who could prove, with a finished vehicle, that the task could be done in a completely different manner.

So in order to provide the would-be restorer or builder with the most comprehensive range of solutions, I have combined my knowledge of restoring two woodies over an eleven-year period with words of wisdom and advice from a wide range of sources. These have included some of the best known professionals and a diverse assortment of home-restorers on both sides of the Atlantic.

In completing my research I have visited a number of workshops and garages, and while the size, shape and facilities varied considerably, I found a universal passion for crafting wood that I have never found in any metal-bashing environment.

Working with wood is an art form that doesn't come naturally to every-

Working with wood develops a passion that will be found in no other workshop or garage.

Wooden bodywork is virtually an art form in its own right, and the finished vehicle can become a thing of amazing beauty.

body, which is why this book provides builders and restorers with solutions that should match their skill and experience levels. Some may have the skill-set and enthusiasm to tackle a complete body rebuild, while others may have to farm out the work to a skilled professional in order to end up with a vehicle that meets their expected restoration standards.

So whatever your requirements, I hope that you will find this eclectic mix of views, techniques and solutions useful, and while some sections of the book may contain a number of alternative suggested fixes, I sincerely hope that you will find one that best suits your needs.

Colin Peck

CHAPTER 1

Types of Vehicle Covered

The art of coachbuilding encompasses a wide range of vehicle types, so I decided from the outset that as many variations as possible would be included in this book, since many of the techniques used and skills required are fundamentally the same, except perhaps in the area of size or scale. So by bringing together such a diverse range of vehicle body styles and their relative restoration processes, the reader will benefit from the experiences of the widest selection of experts ever brought together in one volume.

This chapter comprises a brief photographic description of the types of vehicle covered in these pages.

COACHBUILT CAR BODIES

The elegant and streamlined designs of the 1930s, which often mimicked developments in the aero industry, were a radical departure from the box-like vehicles of the 1920s.

RIGHT: AC was one of the many small car builders that used wood-framed coachbuilt bodies until the late 1950s.

This 1935 Daimler 15 with Mulliner sports saloon bodywork is typical of the 1930s coachbuilders' art.

Just like AC, Allard also used wood framing on its sedans and sports cars

WOODIES

This category includes wooden-bodied station wagons, estate cars and shooting brakes.

BELOW: The Ford Motor Company was one of the first car makers to bring the wooden-bodied station wagon to the masses, both in the USA and the UK.

The Rolls-Royce 20/25 is the epitome of the shooting-brake era of the 1920s and 1930s when such vehicles were built specifically to transport wealthy visitors to hunting lodges and game reserves.

Lancia was one of the few European automakers to offer a wooden-bodied vehicle.

Immediately following the cessation of hostilities across Europe in 1945, Britain witnessed a period of austerity, coupled with a shortage of metal and the introduction of a 30 per cent purchase tax on all new cars. Car dealers and suppliers found a loophole by constructing wooden-bodied utility vehicles that were classified as commercial vehicles and were therefore exempt from tax. This 1948 Healey was one of seventeen such vehicles bodied by Dobbs.

VANS

RIGHT: *Many early vans were built on car chassis, such as this diminutive Austin Seven*

The coachbuilders' art could be adapted to a wide variety of body styles, such as this Morris Y-type ambulance.

TRUCK BODIES AND CABS

The 25ft turning circle of the Austin taxicab chassis made the ideal basis for coachbuilt newspaper delivery vans in London during the 1950s.

Even mass-produced trucks with steel cabs had bodywork constructed from wood right up to the 1970s.

Coachbuilt truck cabs allowed transport operators to adapt them to their operational needs, and they could be easily repaired when damaged.

The very earliest trucks had both bodywork and cabs constructed entirely from wood – some even had doors!

BUSES AND COACHES

Electric-powered trolleybuses replaced tramcars in the UK during the 1930s, and used traditional coachbuilding techniques in their construction.

Wood framing allowed coachbuilders to create some truly artistic designs in low volumes that would not have been economically possible using metal framing.

Petrol- and diesel-powered buses were also constructed extensively with wooden frames during the 1920s, 1930s and 1940s.

NEW-BUILDS OR PHANTOMS

New-build woodies are proving extremely popular in the USA, where car builders are taking models never previously available with a wooden body and building unique vehicles.

This Canadian new-build features sheet metal from a 1950s Morris Oxford combined with woodwork in the style of a Pontiac woodie.

This woodie van was built on an Austin A40 body in Australia.

Even the Citroën 2CV could be rebuilt as a woodie.

Ford never built a Sportsman convertible on the 1939–40 models, so Eric Johnson, from Treehouse Woods in Florida, built his own.

Chrysler Corp never built a Town & Country sedan on its Plymouth range, but that didn't stop this owner from creating one.

This little Austin Seven Special now sports wooden boat-tail bodywork.

This Railton started life as a drophead coupé, but after falling into disrepair was given a new lease of life by being re-bodied as a woodie.

CHAPTER 2

How to Buy – Choosing the Right Vehicle

The purchase of any motor vehicle with a wooden body frame is not something to consider lightly. With steel bodywork on cars, vans, trucks and buses becoming mainstream during the 1940s and 1950s, there's a strong possibility that many of today's auto restorers will have only a limited previous experience, or none at all, of either the delights or the pitfalls of working with wood. So 'buyer beware'!

During the fifteen years that this author has been restoring and owning woodies, I've seen a great many wooden-bodied vehicles that have been snapped up by eager buyers, keen to have their first experience of restoring something different – only to put the vehicle back up for sale a few months later when they realized the amount of work, time and cost involved in turning the vehicle back into anything like its original condition.

It's far too easy to be blinded by the potential value of a restored vehicle without a full appreciation of the work involved in turning a 'project' vehicle into a thing of beauty and a pleasure to own and drive. I've always tried to remove the 'rose-coloured glasses' when going to view a potential purchase, but even years of experience of buying the good, the bad and the downright ugly have sometimes failed to stop me buying the proverbial 'lemon'.

So, rather than just reflecting on my personal criteria for checking out a vehicle prior to purchase, I have sought the opinions of professional and home restorers on both sides of the Atlantic – and whilst many of their views are diverse, they certainly make a lot of sense. Here are some of their suggestions.

GET THE BASICS RIGHT

Suzy Carr from renowned Southern Californian woodie restorers Wood N'Carr, advises that there are a number of 'basics' that you need to get right when going to look at a prospective project vehicle. The first of these is to make any assessments and judgements based on viewing the actual vehicle and not just photos. This sounds like complete common sense, but it's amazing how many people buy over the internet or from a magazine advert, and rather than travelling to view beforehand, just take a chance that the vehicle will live up to the

By carefully selecting the right project vehicle you can help to reduce the time, cost and effort it will take to build a roadworthy vehicle.

condition that the photos appear to show.

On actually viewing the vehicle, Suzy recommends checking the structural integrity of the chassis and steel floorpan (assuming that it has one), as not only is metal very expensive to repair, but if the vehicle's underpinnings are rusted out then there is really nothing on which to build a new wooden body.

One of the most complicated and expensive parts to repair or replace on a wooden-bodied station wagon are the main roof side headers. Covered in fabric, they are often overlooked during the initial vehicle assessment stage, but the work involved in crafting new ones can sometimes make or break a project. Suzy advises using the butt of a pocket knife to start tapping around the top where it's covered in vinyl. 'If you hear a hollow sound, and not solid wood, that could be a huge expense,' she continues. 'If you need to have new wooden headers made for, say, a 1946–48 Ford, then you are looking at around $5,000 for the pair. These are large items, which include finger joins, so check them very carefully.'

When considering the purchase of a vehicle that obviously needs major bodywork repair, you really need to ask yourself if you have the resources, the enthusiasm, and deep enough pockets to see it through to final completion.

The rarity and desirability of woodies now means that even very dilapidated vehicles are being restored.

Roof side rails are big, heavy and expensive to replace. If tapping reveals a hollow sound then there could be internal decay.

RIGHT: *This amount of woodworm damage will usually indicate a serious loss of structural integrity, and replacement of the entire section will be the only effective remedy.*

Woodworm and bug infestations not only have an unsightly impact on the exterior surface of the wood, but they can also weaken the internal structure and joints.

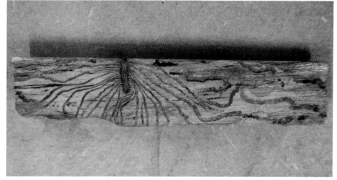

These two pieces of sectioned timber show just how deep woodworm can burrow, and each hole can weaken the entire structure.

WOOD-BORING PESTS

While rot can be a headache, replacement is fairly straightforward. However, this is not the case with any form of bug infestation. Different parts of the world are home to different insects and pests, but any form of wood-boring beetle or bug can wreak havoc with wooden-bodied vehicle structures.

In the UK, woodworm is a common pest. The larval stage of a number of wood-boring beetles thrive in high humidity and poorly ventilated buildings, and while they may not attack a vehicle kept in everyday use, the same cannot be said for one that is put on blocks in a barn and locked away for years.

Peter Baylis, who runs Clanfield Coachbuilding in Oxfordshire in the UK, recommends checking the structural integrity of all joints, especially those in doors, as the residue from the animal and fish glues often used in the coachbuilding trade in the 1940s and 1950s seems a particular favourite of woodworm. This writer has actually purchased woodie doors that initially seemed rigid only to have them 'explode' once any pressure was put on the joints! Woodworm often bore into the joint and devour much of the tenon, leaving it with the tensile strength of honeycomb!

If left unchecked, woodworm attack can lead to serious weakening of structural timber framing and can spoil the appearance of decorative timber, giving it a pock-marked appearance where the bugs have made their escape. Whilst bug attacks on timber are often generally attributed to woodworm, there are other wood-boring pests that can also do damage; these include the common furniture beetle,

death watch beetle, powder post beetle, house longhorn beetle and weevils. All of these are treated in the same way.

Spotting the Tell-Tale Signs

All these insects are beetles, and have a very complex life cycle. Eggs are laid

on the surface of the wood by the adult female beetles, and these hatch out into grubs (larvae) that bore into the wood. It is these grubs (woodworm) that cause damage to the timber. The grubs eventually pupate within the wood and change into adult beetles, which emerge from the wood, mate and lay new eggs to start a new generation.

The time spent in each stage of the life cycle differs for the various insects, and in all cases the damaging grub stage is the longest. The familiar woodworm holes are caused by the adult beetles emerging from the wood.

Attack by wood-boring insects is easily distinguished from other forms of wood deterioration by the

LEFT: Fine dust and powder from when woodworms have exited their bore holes is a tell-tale sign of a potential problem.

BELOW: If you can slip a sharp blade into the wood then rot has surely taken hold and the section needs to be replaced.

distinctive flight holes that appear both on the surface and, if examined, below the surface by the tunnels produced by the larvae.

The adult beetles of the different species can easily be distinguished, but these only live for a short period at certain specific times of the year. The larvae are most difficult to distinguish, and when there are no adults a diagnosis must rely on the nature of the destruction.

Fine wood powder and dust is often a giveaway that something has been chewing at the wood, and Suzy Carr recommends looking for termite 'droppings' along running boards and side mouldings, as this is a classic sign of termite infestation or post-hole beetles. She also suggests taking a small sharp knife and testing whether the blade will slip easily into suspect areas of wood. If it goes in really easily, that could mean fungus or dry rot, and if either of these conditions exists, they both just keep growing on and on, so will need to be cut out to stop the spread.

Unlike the British woodworm, whose exit holes are a sign that the 'pest has left the building' so to speak, termites are not that easily eradicated. So if you do buy a car that is knowingly infested, then it will need to be bagged and fogged, just like a house. Alternatively, if you have access to a large freezer of the type normally used for meat or seafood, putting the woodie into deep freeze for a while should also solve the infestation.

LEARN ALL YOU CAN ABOUT THE VEHICLES

Charles Furman, from the San Diego Woodie Club and chairman of Wavecrest 2011, concurs that many first-time purchasers forego the most important first steps in woodie ownership and then regret it once they realize what they have taken on.

He suggests the following basic rules to ensure that potential purchasers fully understand the vehicles, their values and culture before rushing headlong after the first one that is offered for sale.

1. What types, makes and models are available?

There's no point in rushing in and buy-

The decayed condition of the wood on this Morris Traveller is a clear indication of major structural problems.

A major bug infestation can reduce a woodie wagon to a pile of splinters in no time at all.

ing the first one that comes along – do some research of model types, availability and potential values first in order to set a benchmark.

2. Which models are plentiful and which are rare?

It's essential to know the marketplace.

While the more common models may have a greater following and a good parts supply, will these virtues be reflected in lower values? On the other hand, a rare model may be highly desirable, but will you need to travel to the four corners of the globe to find parts to complete its restoration?

By benchmarking values, and the availability and desirability of the various parts, you can avoid buying a project vehicle that you will perhaps later regret.

Large, rare and high value coachbuilt cars may prove difficult to find spares for.

No matter what the body style is, or was, and whether it's a car, van, truck or bus, the availability of chassis parts has to be a key factor in the decision-making process.

The Morris Minor Traveller was built from 1953 to 1971, and due to the large numbers built is still one of the most numerous and popular woodies available.

3. Which have parts readily available, and which don't?

So what is the main attraction of a wooden-bodied vehicle? Is it the style of the bodywork or the name of the chassis manufacturer? If it's the latter then you need to seriously consider the availability of spare parts.

For example, a mid-1930s Ford car will have a better parts supply chain than, say, a Hudson or a Studebaker, whilst a Rolls-Royce of the same era will have better parts availability than a Hillman or a Jowett: but will the prices be astronomically expensive, and will this cost be reflected in the overall value of the finished vehicle?

4. Some models are more popular than others – so why is that?

Some vehicles are clearly more popular than others, and an understanding of the reasons behind this phenomenon could save you much heartache further down the road. Popularity could be down to large numbers of similar vehicles being available for sale, or perhaps it's because they are cheap and easy to restore. It could also be down to having an active club supporting owners and restorers or maybe because of excellent spares availability. But does popularity also mean that you'll see one at every classic vehicle show from here to Timbuktu, and start to wish you had something a little more special?

5. Which best suits your intended use?

You wouldn't buy a sports car to go off-roading or a double-decker bus when you only needed a taxicab, yet few people buy classic vehicles as a result of considering how they will be used.

If you are building a show vehicle and you'll be the only rider, then maybe two doors and two seats would be plenty, but if there's a need to transport friends and family, and luggage, club regalia or associated products or even pets, then maybe a few extra seats or doors might be in order.

There's also the question of size, and whether it will fit in your garage, as well as the thorny question of engine size and performance. If you never intend to go further than a few local shows and rallies, then a slower performing motor could be all right, but if you intend to make long distance trips then

Do you really need more than two seats?

A bus or coach may meet your needs in terms of passenger carrying capacity, but do you really have room to rebuild or store it?

you'll need to choose a vehicle with the right mechanical specification to avoid thrashing the drive train to within an inch of its life.

Original specification engines are notoriously less powerful and thirstier than modern vehicles, so unless you are considering transplanting modern running gear, you'll need to research drive-line options and data before you buy. While you may be happy to 'adapt' your requirements to the vehicle once it is finished, looking at all the possible usage requirements from the outset could make the difference between ending up with a vehicle that is just acceptable, or one that is fantastic!

6. What are the various types of woodie worth?

While this question is more specific to wooden-bodied station wagons, it could also have some bearing on other types of wooden-bodied vehicles.

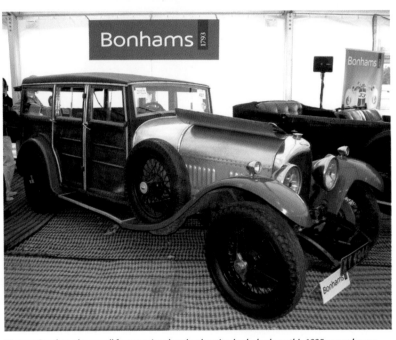

Vintage Bentleys always sell for top prices, but the shooting brake body on this 1925 example was removed soon after it was sold at auction in the UK so that the chassis could be re-bodied as a seemingly more valuable open tourer.

The US surfing scene is intrinsically linked to the woodie culture, which has resulted in these wooden wonders eclipsing the prices of the finest equivalent sedans and convertibles. It has also seen Ford and Mercury woodies become the most desirable and therefore the most valuable.

Prices vary a great deal, so don't go and buy the first vehicle you see for sale. It is important to benchmark condition, desired options and values via the appropriate clubs, such as the National Woodie Club (USA) and the Woodie Car Club (UK), as well as magazine classifieds and internet auctions, and then make an educated decision.

Truck-based woodies are great fun and have a niche following, but generally don't command the same values as car-based woodies.

A modified woodie may be much nicer to drive than an original car, but will it still look original?

For a start, rarity does not always equate to desirability or value. For instance, a vehicle might now be considered rare because it was initially produced in low numbers because it was not particularly well received in the marketplace.

For example, in the USA a fairly rare and high quality 1948 Packard woodie might only be worth $60,000, while a fairly common 1948 Ford woodie in similar condition might be worth twice as much because Fords have a greater following and therefore demand is much higher. Truck-based woodies are also extremely rare, yet are typically less valuable than car-based versions.

7. Original versus modified.
What are the pluses and minuses of a restored original woodie versus a modified woodie? What are the various levels of modification? (Disc brakes, alternators, 12-volt conversions versus modern V-8 engine, automatic transmission and a modern rear-end gearset.)

8. What are the various steps in the restoration process, and what skills are needed to complete them?
A subset of this is honestly assessing your skills in these areas. Are you capable of actually completing the work required to get the vehicle back on the road?

9. Since few backyard restorers actually do everything themselves, it is important to know what various tasks would cost if you had to farm out the work.
Paint, upholstery, chroming, engine

Professionals are usually more than willing to take on any aspect of your restoration project, and it can be immensely useful to identify local resources before you load that project on to your trailer. Many will even be willing to view the project and give you a professional opinion before you make your purchase.

machine shop work and more complex wood working are tasks that are often farmed out.

10. What is restorable and what has to be replaced?
This is a simple enough question, but one that is often overlooked. Assessing what you have got to work with in advance will help you make a fair assessment of the time, money and effort that you will need to put into the project if it's ever going to make it back on to the highway again.

Take the time to realistically assess what can be restored and what needs to be replaced.

Try to look behind and underneath panels to check for bug damage and wood rot, which can be both costly and time-consuming to remedy.

Assessing the condition of wood, sheet metal, chromework, upholstery, glass, tyres, those all-important interior fixtures and mechanical components will, at the very least, enable you to know whether you are paying a fair price for the project vehicle or are letting your head rule your wallet. So you'll at least know in advance if the total cost of restoration will far exceed the price of a newly restored vehicle that's currently for sale!

Rushing out to pick up your first woodie without this knowledge often leads buyers to spend too much money on a woodie that won't meet their needs, that will take four or five times as long to get on the road as they planned, and will cost four or five times as much as they planned, if they get it done at all. Many throw their hands in the air when the costs escalate, and sell the woodie at a fraction of the money they have already invested in the rebuild, for someone else to finish.

THE BIGGER PICTURE

It is important to assess whether you have the required skills, enthusiasm, vision and persistence to see the job completed.

Taking on a vehicle restoration or building project requires the ability to see the big picture, and having the ability to visualize the completed car in your mind is as important as your enthusiasm and excitement about the project, claims Glenn Redding of Ocala, Florida-based Redding Woodworks. Glenn also believes that it is essential to stay with the project until it is finished.

This view is also shared by Jeff Yeagle of Phoenixville, Pennsylvania, who adds:

Knowing what level of project one can handle is critical. While some individuals are willing to go from the 'ground up', others are only willing to maintain their collector car.

As a result a prospective purchaser must look at projects that they can realistically handle, as with every project there is a point where money

must be spent, and the willingness and ability to do so is key to the success of any project. Any project I take on must therefore pass a couple of crucial tests: first, you must be willing to be 'stuck' with the project forever! You must like it enough to want to have it for the remainder of your life, because that's always a real possibility. If you can't

Are you really sure you have the skill and enthusiasm to see a sorry-looking project vehicle through to full restoration?

You'll need the ability to see beyond the rotten wood and rusty metal, and to recognize the vehicle's hidden potential.

answer this question with a yes, then don't even consider the project.

Second, the vehicle should either be very complete, or (in my humble opinion) it should be a Ford. Here in the United States the majority of components for Ford autos are relatively easy to obtain, whereas when considering other marques this does not generally hold true. As a result, if I am approached with a project car it must be complete if it's not a Ford.

In writing this book, I said from the outset that it will explore the workload requirements of the home restorer – the project manager and those who can hand the whole car across to a professional. As a home restorer, Joe

Cocuzza, from north-east Pennsylvania, advises that you need to consider seriously your skill levels before you load the project vehicle on to your trailer.

At the time of writing, Joe is approaching the end of an eleven-year restoration of a 1947 Chrysler Town and Country sedan; he also advises a would-be restorer to check how much money they can afford to sink into the project, as well as the time that it is likely to take to restore the vehicle and the time required to source parts. Obviously the simple solution is to buy a vehicle in the best possible condition, but these may be outside your budget, and with good original vehicles in short supply, the solution for many of us is to take on a project.

It is also suggested that you endeavour to find a vehicle in the most original condition, and as complete a project as possible, because restoring a vehicle to its original condition may be difficult, if not impossible, if too many components are missing. Components for American-built station wagons, such as door latches, handles, window mechanisms and body hardware, are often unique to a particular model year, and can be immensely difficult and expensive to replace.

A woodie that has sat outside in the weeds over a number of years, slowly succumbing to the onslaught of termites or decay, needs to be treated like a crime scene before the carcass is hauled out of the bushes. In such cases you should make an inventory of all hardware from a similar vehicle, if at all possible, and then be prepared to crawl on your knees, cut down the bushes and grass and, if needs be, use a metal detector to locate all that hard-to-replace hardware.

Another area that is often overlooked in the enthusiasm to get your hands on the project vehicle, is how original it is in terms of body style, numbers of seats and doors, and even type of windows and door latches. Time spent researching this information in advance could save a lot of heartache, expense and travel later on: it is a lot easier to restore what you already have at hand than to have to track down, buy, and then restore a part that was missing.

At the outbreak of World War II in Europe in 1939 the British government of the day seconded the entire new stock of auto dealers across the country. In addition, many of the large full-size Canadian-built sedans and convertibles that had previously been so popular in pre-war Britain were hastily converted into ambulances, fire trucks, tow trucks and food delivery trucks. This was usually achieved by cutting off the rear half of the car's bodywork and bolting on some other type of utility bodywork.

At the end of hostilities these were the first vehicles to be disposed of at war surplus sales across Britain, and these 'half cars' proved extremely popular with small coachbuilding firms, which could hastily throw together a wooden-bodied station

Finding a project vehicle that is as complete as possible will drastically reduce the amount of time spent tracking down parts, and the mileages involved in collecting them.

An unmolested original vehicle is a better buy than one that has been torn apart by a previous owner. Even if the bodywork is damaged, at least everything will be in the right place, and you will be able to make patterns from which to build new parts.

Few war-time woodie conversions survive, and those that have are eagerly sought after by military vehicle collectors; however, they don't always have the same potential value as civilian versions.

wagon conversion. However, although built in their thousands, few such conversions exist today, largely because the standard and quality of the workmanship left a lot to be desired. Whilst some were built to a high standard, the majority were produced to fulfil a need for 'new' vehicles in a nation that had been starved of new vehicles for around seven years.

However, it is not unusual for such a vehicle to be described by a seller as 'a unique one-off prototype built at great expense by the original chassis manufacturer'. Obviously this is nonsense, and if acquired for a lot of money the purchaser could later feel justifiably dejected if he discovers that the vehicle was most likely nailed together in somebody's shed.

It is therefore essential to keep an open mind when viewing any project vehicle, and to conduct as much research as you can in advance, from auto clubs, associations and even museums, so that you can make a fair assessment of the history associated with the vehicle.

AVOID DOING THE JOB TWICE

Buying an unfinished project where a previously frustrated restorer has given up halfway through a restoration is not to be undertaken lightly. Taking a car apart yourself, and photographing and documenting everything, is a difficult enough task, but imagine buying a vehicle that has been disassembled by another person, and then trying to piece it back together, assuming that you've got all the parts. It could be like a jigsaw with no box.

Joe Cocuzza remembers meeting somebody who was restoring another Chrysler Town and Country Sedan.

He told me that when he bought the car it was 60–70 per cent restored/completed. He also said that he would never do that again as he wound up tearing the whole thing apart again because he was not happy with the workmanship of the guy who owned the car before him. So why do things twice if you don't have to?

Whereas many restorers recommend trying to estimate in advance how much time a project will take, and then making sure that you have both the financial and time resources available to see it through, Joe controversially advises would-be restorers not to go down the estimating route: 'Such an estimate usually gets proven to be a fallacy really quickly, and that is what leads to the frustration that often results in unfinished projects. Realize the task in front of you is a difficult one,

An acute shortage of new vehicles on the home front in post-war Britain, coupled with restrictions on the availability of raw materials such as metal, saw a number of small British coachbuilders turn their skills to re-bodying surplus military vehicles.

Buying an unfinished project may allow you to sidestep a lot of the hard work, sleepless nights and skinned knuckles normally associated with the tear down process. However, the project vehicle may now contain bodged repairs and badly rebuilt components and may even be missing major components. So 'buyer beware'!

and once you commit to it make sure you don't fail.'

Whichever route you choose to follow when it comes to assessing the potential cost of a rebuild or newbuild, be prepared to do the very best job you can and try to avoid cutting corners – they will always show and detract from your overall pleasure in the finished vehicle.

On a vehicle where the framework will be hidden from view, or clad in some sort of wood, metal or fabric panels, matching grain will not be an issue. However, it will be a big issue on a woodie, and ensuring that all the grain is of a consistent pattern and a similar colour can be both a time- and a cash-consuming exercise.

BE AWARE OF VALUES

While most of us will build or restore a vehicle for personal reasons, common sense dictates that we also need to conduct a reality check on potential values. While some of the vehicles covered by this book will be common enough to have benchmarked market values, many others will be so rare or unique that they may be difficult to value definitively. However, if you take emotion out of the equation you would surely not spend $40,000 to restore a vehicle that was only worth $20,000 – especially if you could go out the next day and buy a show winner for $20,000!

Bodywork restoration owes little to the value or kudos of the chassis it's mounted on, and it's very easy to pay Rolls-Royce prices to restore an Alvis, Austin, Ford or Chevrolet. However, knowing which one could be the most cost-effective project means you won't feel too bad if somebody later offers you a fully restored vehicle for less than the money you've put into your project.

As Joe Cocuzza concludes, 'Buy with your brain and not your heart.'

So, putting aside the considerations of which chassis manufacturer is your preferred choice, the added considerations when buying a wooden-bodied classic vehicle can be summed up under two headings: the condition of the architectural wood and the condition of the structural wood.

Condition of the Architectural Wood

One could argue that all wood on a wooden-bodied vehicle is in some way structural. For instance, those plywood insert panels certainly add to the structural integrity of the body when glued, screwed or nailed into place. However, the fact that they can be removed relatively easily means that they are not crucial elements of the vehicle's structure, and so need not necessarily be a deal breaker.

The fact that a previous owner didn't even bother to try to match the colour of the stain or varnish means that the quality of this repair is exceedingly suspect.

Heavy staining on the plywood panels is a good indicator that the vehicle has previously been stored in damp conditions, so check the joints and the general condition of the hardwood frame for wood rot and wet damage.

This car has suffered extensive decay to the rear due to being stored for a number of years with the rear of the body exposed to the elements. However, a detailed examination may reveal that the rest of the body is structurally sound and restorable.

Exposed woodwork has to be revarnished every few years to retain protection from the elements, because once decay sets in, things can turn ugly very quickly.

It takes many years, if not decades, of exposure to the elements for ash framing to turn grey and decompose like this, and it could be an indicator that the vehicle has terminal bodywork decay, thus requiring complete replacement.

Condition of the Structural Wood

Structural members such as the door posts, door frames, roof supports and the tailgate frame are a different matter. These require significant investment in time, material and equipment in order to replace them. Repairs can be carried out, but considerable time can be spent finding wood grain that is a perfect match for an exposed frame. Also, unless a repair is carried out properly it can weaken the frame, thus putting the whole structure in jeopardy.

If you know your choice of vehicle is likely to be expensive, and so you are preparing to take on a total body rebuild, then you might as well go for a basket case, advises Eric Johnson, who runs Treehouse Woods in Cocoa Beach, Florida. 'But make sure it's as complete as you can get, as hardware is extremely hard to find,' he adds.

Metal brackets and door latches are the hardest parts to find if they are missing and can command high prices, if they can be found at all. Eric has been making new pattern parts for Ford woodies for some time, but is now selective as to whom he sells them, as he has found that some people have been buying them and then selling them on eBay as original Ford parts.

Eric continues:

You've got to figure out your own capabilities in terms of shop expertise, project management and even finances before you start. Talk to professional restorers first, as most will be more than happy to tell what needs restoration so that you go into the project with your eyes open – and don't stop once you've started, as the longer the restoration takes, the more money it will cost you.

As you've probably already gathered, the acquisition of a wooden-bodied vehicle as a restoration project is not something to rush into, and some may question their own ability to make a sound judgement on what is a worthwhile proposition and what is an absolute waste of effort. Therefore it's worth considering taking an experienced vehicle owner or restorer along with you to view the vehicle ahead of purchase.

If you don't know anybody suitably experienced, then contact the appropriate vehicle club as they will almost certainly have a club member local to you who could help with advice and/ or an inspection. And don't be afraid to offer to pay the expenses involved in getting expert help with the inspection, as it could save much heartache later on.

Charles Furman, from the San Diego Woodie Club, comments:

I will probably never buy another woodie without consulting with some of my woodie expert friends. And if you don't have any woodie expert friends, then hire one. Take a reputable woodie restorer, professional or backyard restorer with you, to assess the woodie of your dreams, even if it costs you a few hundred dollars, pounds or euros.

Once you have selected a make, model and a body style that you believe meets your intended use, then double check that it's in the right price range. You need to look long and hard at the overall condition of the vehicle, and don't fall in love with how it looks in a photograph or on the internet, or how it looks from twenty feet away.

Examine the condition of everything you can possibly check. Everything that is not in perfect condition has a cost associated with it in terms of money, labour and time. By assessing the condition of each component (wood body, metal panels and substructure, chromework, interior, mechanical components, electrical components, tyres and so on) and determining the true cost in time and money that it will take

Hardware is often unique to a particular model type and can be extremely difficult, and expensive, to source if missing from the project vehicle.

US-built Ford woodies use exposed metal brackets to tie the roof to the body frame, and most are unique to a specific model year.

Individual coachbuilders often had their own unique method of attaching doors, and although many used generic coachbuilders' hinges, these are now difficult to source. Good quality period hinges tend to be brass, and substantial in construction, so don't expect to find replacements at the local home improvement store.

In many cases it will be more cost effective to build a new body frame than to try and repair a rotten original.

to bring them up to good condition, you will begin to get a realistic picture of whether or not this woodie is for you.

Chip Kussmaul of automotive woodworking specialists Cincinnati Woodworks, has this to say:

Perhaps the most important thing to consider is that rot tends to happen from within the wood, and moves outwards. That's because the rot needs moisture, and the moisture is on the inside. I've seen wooden parts that look just fine externally, but had almost literally nothing more than a veneer of sound-looking wood, with nothing but sawdust on the inside. Tapping with a knuckle and listening for a hollow sound can at least give a clue. So

Make sure the project vehicle is as complete as possible, even if it means crawling through the undergrowth looking for missing brackets and unique hardware.

Many projects are advertised as a 'bare bones' vehicle – ask the vendor if they have any parts hidden away in a garage or barn, perhaps taken off many years before and forgotten about.

Transporting your crumbling project to your home garage, or perhaps to a local bodyshop, needs careful planning so as not to lose any parts along the way.

If the bodywork is suffering from terminal decay, then you may have to brace the roof or side panels with wooden supports to stop the remaining bodywork collapsing the first time the transporter goes over a bump or pothole.

deliberately. When I'm working on a car I'm not too familiar with, I try to disassemble one side of the car while leaving the other side untouched. Then as I proceed I can easily take whatever measurements I need (including diagonals!) from the complete side, while I work on the other.

So as you can see, there are a number of different views on what you should look for in a project vehicle, but each and every one is valid and hopefully can help steer you in the right direction. Jeff Boyd, who runs a woodie restoration shop in northern California, advises: 'Do have a plan B if you bite off more than you can chew, however I hope that the contents of this book will help most readers to produce the wooden-bodied vehicle they aspire to own.'

Suzy Carr adds:

I'd advise checking the obvious points such as joints and where water could collect.

While a metal car can have rusted areas cut out and replaced with good new steel, wood doesn't offer that ease of repair. Generally, the entire part has to be replaced if any section of it is bad. And that can easily require full disassembly. So because of the work involved, my view is that, in practical terms, a vehicle that needs 20 per cent or more of its wooden structure replaced should probably just have it all replaced.

Speaking of replacement, do it very

If somebody asked me what I would recommend to look for when buying a woodie, I'd flip the question and ask them where they intended to start from. For instance, are they considering a fully restored car that is 'finished', or perhaps a restoration project, or even something halfway between the two?

Transporting a vehicle with rotten bodywork requires a gentle touch. Be prepared to wrap, tie, bind and even chain parts to the transporter so that it arrives at its destination with everything you loaded. Clean plastic sheeting can be used to help keep things together. If a third party is undertaking the transport, be prepared to oversee the loading so that fragile bodywork is not further damaged by a heavy-handed truck driver.

Don't underestimate the weight of the project vehicle. Most family-sized cars will struggle to haul safely a large trailer and a vehicle, perhaps with a combined weight of 3 tonnes (6,000lb) or more. In many countries there are strict towing capacity weight limits, so you will need a heavyweight truck to carry the vehicle or haul it on a trailer.

Wherever you intend to start from, do extensive research of the vehicle type and model, and find potential restorers and get ballpark costs before you buy. It's also advisable to check out if the chosen restorer has worked on similar models before, as this could have a major impact on cost, and the resulting quality of work.

Lastly, I'm always surprised when people buy cars remotely, without ever seeing them until a truck arrives at their house, garage or workshop to unload. You really must go and see any potential purchase beforehand, as photos just don't do a vehicle justice, and flaws and defects are all too easy to disguise with modern photo-editing software.

The last word on the subject comes from Ron Heiden, who concludes: 'You want the vehicle to have as many original parts as possible, as buying replacements can be expensive. Window-winding mechanisms, door locks, handles, hinges and so on, can be very hard to find and exceedingly expensive.'

GETTING IT HOME IN ONE PIECE

One of the often-overlooked aspects of tackling a restoration project is the problem faced with actually transporting the crumbling wreck home without losing too many parts en route. We've already talked about inspecting the bodywork with a view to restoration problems, and we've touched on checking that all the unique hardware is with the vehicle, but it's equally essential to ensure that parts that were on the body when it started its journey are still there when it finally arrives home.

Doors could be taped or wired shut, and any loose parts should either be made secure or removed altogether and placed inside the towing vehicle. Woodwork that has badly decayed and will ultimately be replaced could be made more secure by nailing or screwing on additional timber supports to ensure that it stays together on the journey.

It would be bad enough to have parts fall off the trailer or tow truck, and possibly cause damage to following vehicles, but with a lot of surviving wood-framed vehicles – particularly those that were coachbuilt – it is essential to retain as much of the original bodywork as possible for future pattern making.

So if the rear tailgates part company with the rest of the body after you hit a pothole and then get run over by an eighteen-wheeler, you'll end up having to guess what the back end really looked like.

In some cases it will not be possible or appropriate to start nailing a support framework to the prized bodywork, however it may be possible to wrap it in plastic sheeting, or even to use the expanded plastic mesh often used on construction sites or roadworks. You may even be able to throw a tarpaulin or dust sheet over the vehicle to help keep it together, but whatever you do you've got to keep in mind that many of the parts – especially the hardware – might be almost impossible to replace.

CHAPTER 3

Tools and Workshop Health and Safety

KEEP IT SAFE

Working on any vehicle has its dangers, but wooden-bodied vehicles have their own inherent levels of risk, and you cannot skimp on health and safety precautions. As a general rule, there is no safety device that is more useful than just plain common sense. However, when working with saws, chisels, grinders and sanders, not forgetting various chemicals that carry their own inherent dangers, you cannot take your personal safety seriously enough.

Having sufficient work space is a key requirement for working on any motor vehicle, but when building or restoring a wooden-bodied vehicle you will need sufficient space to remove part, if not all of the bodywork, as well as space for the various machines to make the new parts. The more space restrictions you have around where you are working, the greater the possibility of accidents. Working with power tools in a restricted space is a recipe for disaster!

One area that is often overlooked by the home restorer is that sawdust is not only extremely harmful to your respiratory system, but it is also highly flammable! Most professional workshops will have some sort of dust extraction system, and while most home restorers may choose not to go down this route for a single restoration project, it is certainly worth considering such an installation if you plan to build a second or third vehicle.

A good quality face mask is essential when sanding or grinding wood. Most power sanders now come with a dust-catching system, but if you are 'going

So assuming you now have your project vehicle sitting in your garage or workshop, just where do you start?

Having sufficient working space is a key element to keeping things safe.

Even if you have a small home workshop or garage, keeping everything clean and tidy will help to keep the working environment safe and accident free.

old school' then why not try sanding outside? Don't let the sawdust collect on surfaces as that could still be in the air when you are not sanding and the face mask is removed, so brush the surfaces regularly, sweep the floor and, if you have the luxury of an air compressor, use the air gun to blast the surfaces clean – making sure you are wearing your face mask before you start blasting!

I personally like to keep the work area as clean as possible so that there's nothing to slip on, fall on me whilst I'm working on the car, or have land on my freshly varnished woodwork.

The only fire I've ever had in my garage was when some sparks from an angle grinder landed on a pack of wire wool I had under the bench, causing it to combust. Fortunately it was only a small fire, but that wire wool really does burn, and it glows red hot like a camp fire, making it difficult to stamp out. I now keep two fire extinguishers to hand, one attached to the workbench and the other permanently inside my woodie.

Not only is sawdust highly flammable, but so are many of the chemicals, paints and solvents used in the restoration process, and we could all learn a lesson from the professionals, such as Suzy Carr from Wood N'Carr. She advises:

We have the local fire department carry out an inspection in our work-

shop and on fire extinguishers every twelve months, as we take the risks very seriously. We also hold team safety meetings once a month where we go through any safety issues.

We also promote cleanliness, and once a week we dedicate thirty minutes before closing to carrying out a super-clean, and encouraging the team to make sure that all tools are put away so we have a neat and tidy working environment.

Whilst our main focus is on restoration and building techniques, we should not overlook health hazards associated with the pre-build process, such as the making of templates. You will probably be using the best materials available for the finished build, but it stands to reason that you will probably use cheaper materials for templates and mock-ups.

Depending on where you live, what the weather is like and how much work space you have, you may choose to sand, saw or router inside or outside. But wherever you choose, make sure you use a good quality face mask to avoid the risk of respiratory problems, and if sanding inside, remember that sawdust is highly flammable.

Sanding outside can reduce mess in your workshop, but do remember that the noise of power tools can annoy your neighbours.

35

Many restorers will use whatever is to hand for the mock-up process, such as plywood or even MDF (medium density fibreboard). However, whilst plywood is relatively safe to work with, the dust from MDF is extremely unpleasant. Not only is it an irritant to throat and nose, but the dust is incredibly powder-like and invasive, so it is essential to wear a good quality face mask when working with this material. One of the main problems with MDF is that like all fibreboards, formaldehyde resins are used to bond together the constituent parts. This is usually urea formaldehyde, but some fibreboards including exterior or marine quality board will use stronger glues, such as phenol formaldehyde.

Even at a low level, exposure to formaldehyde through inhalation can cause irritation to the eyes, nose, throat and mucous membranes. Formalde-hyde can also affect the skin, leading to dermatitis, and the respiratory system causing asthma and rhinitis. So don't take any chances – in fact I would recommend that you keep clear of MDF altogether and only use plywood for mock-up work.

Another product from which to protect yourself is epoxy, and particularly its dust. We will be covering the use of this product in detail in Chapter 15, but it's worth mentioning here that once you are overexposed to epoxy, you become hypersensitive and then need to forget about using this wonderful material ever again.

Working with wood, no matter how you choose to tackle the work, will almost certainly entail the use of power tools with plenty of high-speed rotating parts. Whilst some professionals choose to remove the safety guards, this is not a practice that I can condone and should be avoided at all cost. Any machinery with moving parts can be dangerous, so you can minimize the risk of personal injury by not wearing loose clothing, hanging jewellery, mobile (cell) phone headsets or music earpieces anywhere near such machinery.

Gloves can give protection, but can also harbour a measure of risk if worn at the wrong time. I regularly use disposable latex gloves when sanding, varnishing and generally keeping my hands clear of dirt or grime. However, I know from personal experience that they should not be worn near high-speed machines after getting a gloved hand too near a wire brush attachment on a high speed drill. Whilst the thin latex may have protected my skin from the initial impact with the steel wires, the glove was shredded instantly and the shreds torn from the glove continued

One of the most popular and useful tools for any woodworker is the router. However, good quality ear defenders will help reduce any long-term effects to your hearing.

Many woodworkers make their router jigs for cutting specific angles or shapes, but a good quality depth gauge is an absolute must for accurate bit (blade) settings.

Richard McCloskey is seen here machining a double/curved top mortise in the front, passenger-side hinge-board of a Ford 'shoebox' woodie. He is utilizing a large mounting fixture to hold in place the piece being routed, while using a home-made jig/fixture to run the router against for accuracy.

Chip Kussmaul of Cincinnati Woodworks is seen here using a pin router to machine a slot in part of the lower rail of a Chrysler Town and Country trunk lid. The wood is oversized and only gets cut to final size after all the slots and tenons are cut. Chips tells us, 'The router bit is pretty much buried in the wood and this is my second pass as it's only a ¼in bit and it would break if I tried to cut full depth in a single pass.'

Steve at Cincinnati Woodworks is using a jig to do the 'scooping' operation on a corner post. The router sled rides on two curved rails, and the template is screwed into place to make sure the scooping only happens where it is supposed to. The router has a template guide ring.

It is essential to let the router cut at a speed appropriate to the depth of the wood. If you try to push the router bit too hard you can burn the wood, as seen here, and also run the risk of equipment damage or failure, and possible injury.

A quality router can be the woodworker's best friend if handled correctly. Here Ron Heiden demonstrates his skill on a securely clamped section of wood.

to rotate at something like 2,000rpm, lashing my skin like a rotating whip. So be warned!

There are also key health and safety considerations when dealing with stripping and sanding, the making and assembly of new bodywork, and stain-

ing and varnishing the finished woodwork, but we'll cover those under the appropriate sections.

Lastly, let us not forget cleanliness. Dirt, dust and grime can spoil the appearance and reliability of any project, but even more importantly,

they can be a hazard in the workshop as we've already outlined. However, cleanliness should also extend to keeping the workspace clear of wood offcuts, spillages, loose tools and cables. I always remove all tools, parts and equipment from the floor of the workshop whenever I've finished work for the day as slips and trips are 'caused', and not accidents.

I also always make a point of sweeping out the workshop floor at least once a week, and will often use my compressed air gun to dust down the car, floor, workbench and all those little nooks and crannies where that unique nut or part always rolls when you are halfway through a rebuild.

TAKING THINGS APART

Before you jump right in and start disassembling the vehicle, you might also want to think about drawing up a list of specialist tools and equipment that you are going to need to turn this pile of rotting timbers and delaminating

Wood N'Carr undertakes a once-a-week 'super-clean' of their workshop in Signal Hill, and I'd recommend doing the same, wherever you work.

plywood back into a thing of beauty. Ensuring you have the right tools to do the job might just save you getting halfway through the tear-down process, finding you don't have the right tool, and using a hammer, screwdriver or chisel to force something and then irreparably damaging it.

In seeking opinions from professionals and home restorers, I've been amazed at the different viewpoints on what tools you really need to take apart and then build and craft a wooden vehicle body. Some point towards a fully equipped workshop as the only way to go, whilst others get by with just a few basic tools – having produced some fine vehicles to back up their comments.

You'd be most unlikely to tackle an engine transplant and then discover when everything was unbolted that you'd not given any thought as to how you were actually going to lift the engine block out of the vehicle. So it is with a wooden-bodied vehicle, and by looking at the tools and equipment you might need at the end of the job you could also be identifying tools you might just need at the beginning.

However, most of the tools you'll need at the beginning will be needed for the stripping-down and disassembling stage (unless of course you've acquired a vehicle with a body that's already been devoured by termites, or you are building a new-build vehicle). So let's start with those.

Obviously a good selection of sharp flat-blade and cross-head screwdrivers is essential. I've also found that an impact driver with a good selection of screwdriver heads can also prove useful for stubborn screws. However, it is important to be careful not to use too much force as you can easily damage the wood.

Removing Steel Screws

Most wooden frames used a combination of joints, such as tenons and finger joints, coupled with screws for rigidity … and they usually weren't built with a view to be taken apart again within the builder's lifetime. So regular steel screws were most commonly used to hold the frame together, and over the years these tend to form a rust bond with the wood, making them very

difficult to remove without damaging the wood or the screw.

Such screws need to be approached with caution, as an over-zealous use of power tools can easily remove the screw head, or part of it, making it very

Make sure you have the right tools for the job before you start taking the bodywork apart.

Covering the area around a damaged screw head with masking tape can help protect the wood should you need to resort to a more heavy-handed method of screw removal, such as an impact driver. Try tightening it first, as this often helps to break it free, before trying to unscrew it.

A micro heat gun can be useful for loosening stubborn screws, but treat them with gentle respect otherwise you will burn the wood.

difficult to remove. I usually start by assessing the quality of the wood to be removed in terms of whether I want to save it. Assuming that I do want to re-use that particular piece of wood, then I'll follow a number of steps to try to remove the screw without damaging the wood.

I usually start by sticking strips of masking tape (the kind you'd use to tape off areas when spray painting) around the screw head. This can reduce the risk of damaging the surface of the wood if the screwdriver blade slips as a result of too much pressure being applied. If the screw won't budge I'll then slip on a pair of eye protectors, and switch from manual to power tools in the form of an electric drill/screwdriver and use the substantial torque to try to shock it free after first tightening and then untightening the screw. If that doesn't shift it, I'll put on the heavy gloves and try the impact driver, once again tightening the screw first (to shock it free) and then trying to loosen it.

If the screw stubbornly remains firm, another possible solution is to use the fine flame jet from one of those hand-held micro heat guns that most big hardware stores carry for soldering. With a steady hand you can heat the head and shank of the screw without burning the surrounding wood, and this may help to break the screw free. But be warned, if you are not confident in holding the small flame jet directly on the screw head, then perhaps this is not the best method for you!

Depending on access to the screw head and how it is holding the wooden joint together, you may be able to drill the head of the screw off by using a small drill bit. However, I've found that this method can often break small drill bits as they catch easily on the screw head, and if you use too much pressure, pieces of the drill bit can fly off. So wear eye protectors and keep your fingers clear of the drill.

The worst screws will have rusted away to almost nothing just under the head, while the thread has grown a large ball if rust debris is locking it in place. These usually break, leaving the threaded section of the screw buried. A small hole drilled alongside it will allow you to dig it out, and then the hole can be plugged with new wood glued in.

If all else fails you may have to resort to trying to slip a chisel, or similar flat-bladed tool, between the joint of the wood, and this may just break the screw's hold. As a last resort you may be able to force the two wooden surfaces apart enough to slide a flat saw blade between and cut the end of the screw off, thus releasing the joint.

One of my favourite pieces of equipment in the garage is my trusty air compressor, and the general purpose air gun is ideal for cleaning out debris from screws and screw holes, but also for blasting decades of gunge and rubbish out of joints. This can often give you a clearer picture of the ends of screws and bolts, so you can see exactly what's holding the bodywork together.

In general, the tools for taking the wooden body apart are fairly basic, but remember to take your time, and don't use too much force even if you think you'll never need that moth-eaten piece of wood again, because you may just need it as a template later on, and may then regret your over-zealous use of a crowbar or club hammer.

WORKING WITH NEW WOOD

As to the tools and equipment that are needed to build a vehicle body, the first thing to remember is that you are dealing with thick hardwoods, so the cheap, bottom-of-the-line tools that you might have in the garage for the occasional DIY job around the house quite literally won't cut them. Even some of the home workshop brands are not really up to the job of sawing large pieces of ash or maple.

However, many of the professionals I've spoken to are more than happy to help out home restorers, whether to rough cut a large section of framework or perhaps to shape and finish just a single section. So go and ask a professional for help if you are stuck, rather than trying to force a tool to go beyond its design parameters.

Obviously a lot can be achieved with hand tools, provided you are willing to invest the time and effort to achieve a result that you could probably achieve in minutes if you use a power tool. All the people who have supplied their personal recommendations for this book have different views on what makes the perfect tool and equipment

Steve Foreman and his son James (below left) of Woodies – the UK's largest supplier of woodwork for Morris Minor Travellers – believes that the subject of tools can be defined as tools and equipment you'd really like to have, and tools and equipment you need to do the job.

combination, but at least their views should guide you in the right direction.

Chip Kussmaul, from Cincinnati Woodworks, rightly states that precision is important, so quality, powerful tools are the way to go. 'Avoid radial arm saws,' he advises, 'because even the industrial grade ones are difficult to keep true. Where possible, use a table saw instead, as even a medium duty machine can do wonderful things.'

Chip also advises making sure you're using appropriate tooling:

There are a million types of blades and bits available, so make sure your tooling is appropriate to what you're doing. Also, make sure you've got the correct rpm. Since good tools and tooling cost serious money, see what you can find on Craigslist and suchlike. Tools were generally better made fifty years ago than they are today. My bandsaw is nearly a hundred years old, and there is nothing made today that can replace it.

A good quality bandsaw is one of the essential tools for cutting hardwoods, but it can be extremely dangerous if used incorrectly. Always ease the wood on to the blade – never force it. Whilst some professionals may be comfortable to forego safety glasses and ear protectors, our advice is to use them all the time.

We don't use CNC machines either, as we do everything on an individual basis. We also have lots of hand tools, such as routers, sanders, cordless screwdrivers, hand blocks, chisels and so on – in fact, just what you would expect to find in a well equipped woodworking shop.

Steve Foreman of Woodies has listed the tools and machines he believes you really need to build a wooden-bodied vehicle, in approximate order of importance:

◆ Bandsaw (as big and as powerful as you can afford)
◆ Surface thicknesser
◆ Large hand-held router
◆ Smaller but powerful hand-held router
◆ Spindle router
◆ Belt and drum sanders
◆ Table saw or compound angle cross-cut saw
◆ The usual selection of hand tools and chisels
◆ Chainsaw for cutting raw material into suitable lengths

You may also wish to make your own jigs and guides for working with the bandsaw. Here we see a jig constructed by Gary Tuffnell at Classic Restorations. This wooden jig has a round edge and allows Gary to cut curved pieces in a constant arc and at a set width.

Chip's basic tool and equipment list includes an air compressor, sandpaper, wood bleach, scrapers, jigs, clamps and glue, and its simplicity is echoed by Suzy Carr, of Wood N'Carr in California, who states:

We don't have anything fancy here! Some of the equipment we use includes table saws, very large band saws, overhead mill, wall-mounted saws, boring machines – and no shaper, as we feel they are too dangerous.

Ron Thomas from Washington State found he needed to create more than 120 individual pieces to restore his 1948 Oldsmobile correctly.

Having the right tools for the job is key to producing a result that is both structurally sound and aesthetically pleasing, and whilst the capital cost of some of the required equipment may add substantially to the cost of the vehicle build, trying to cut corners can often lead to poor quality workmanship and the possibility of accidents. For instance, spending around £250 on a bench morticer for making joints and paring workpieces may seem excessive for something you might only use a few times during the vehicle build. However, using a modified drill press may not provide the level of accuracy or neatness required. This, in turn, can lead to machine tools being put under stress, which can lead to accidents.

The great thing about wooden-bodied vehicles is that they are not really that difficult to work with, provided that the individual restorer either has some basic knowledge of machinery or is willing to learn – just as where the professionals will offer different suggestions and viewpoints on tool selection, so it is with the home restorer. For instance, when Ron Thomas from Washington State started working on the woodwork of two 1948 Oldsmobile woodies he had acquired for restoration, he began to realize that this was a woodworking undertaking that could be beyond his abilities, both in time and skill. He tells us:

> I had developed woodworking skills by building several boats and houses, but this task required fabrication of more than 120 different pieces to precision replication. While visiting Rick Mack's workshop, I observed the hundreds of router patterns that he had collected, many for making the parts on my cars. Terror began to set in, as the hand-held router is my least favourite tool.
>
> However, I had read about the CNC router in *Woodenboat* magazine, and found that the Shopbot CNC router seemed to be ideal for the task in hand. It took a while to convince me that a ½in router bit could cut ash at 3in per second with repeatable precision. However, I had spent the past twenty years as an engineer, and felt comfortable with the design and tool path technology, so the Shopbot 48 × 96PRT Alpha CNC router was purchased and set up with a 5hp spindle.

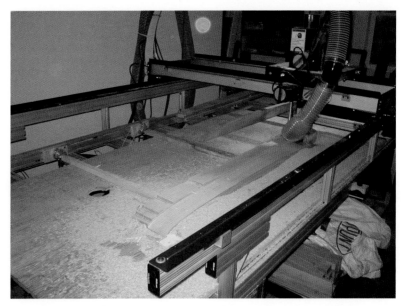

Ron used a Shopbot Alpha CNC router table to trace and shape all the parts he needed for his Oldsmobile woodie.

> I used the machine to trace, with a probe, the shapes and profiles of my original (usually rotten) parts. Using the probe points, I could make a virtual model of the part in Rhino 3D CAD design software. From the CAD model, I'd make 2D and 3D toolpaths using the Shopbot Partswork software. This process meant that there was a lot of hand fitting and finishing, but I could work on those parts whilst the CNC machine was cutting.
>
> I have finished one of the cars and have parts for two more. The woodwork actually became easier and less time-consuming than the chassis, engine and upholstery work. Most wouldn't choose this technique, but it has worked for me.

Like most things in life, the more experienced you are, the easier the job becomes, which is why many of the leading professionals are able to turn out high-quality work without having their workshops packed to the hilt with every conceivable woodworking machine and gizmo.

One of the legends in the world of woodie restoration in southern California is Ron Heiden, who has a small but perfectly formed workshop in Leucadia. Ron has been turning out show-winning woodies for many years with tools that include electric plane, electric grinder, hand plane, router, belt sander, bandsaw, and a table saw on which he can skilfully cut finger joints.

STAYING MOTIVATED

It can be frustrating keeping the motivation going when restoring a vehicle, particularly when you reach the 75 per cent complete mark – so close, yet so far! It is important not to rush jobs or to cut corners and not fully complete certain jobs just to bring the car nearer to completion. If you go down this route you'll almost certainly regret it later and will probably end up tearing things apart again to do the job right.

An acceptance that many people have run the course before you can be of help. They may have found the same frustrations, but stopping to ensure the particular job in hand has been done properly and completely is the best course of action. It can often help to look back at the progress made to date for reassurance that the project is heading in the right direction.

Sliding bevels are great for measuring angles and transferring them to templates, but sometimes you need really big ones. Try making your own.

CHAPTER 4

Dismantling, Cataloguing and Storing Parts

The old line about 'Fools rush in' springs to mind when tackling the subject of how to take a vehicle apart so that you know how to put it back together again. Problems with the reassembly of popular steel-bodied cars or vans can usually be overcome by examining the panel work on a similar vehicle or possibly even an owner's manual.

However, even if you are lucky enough to have access to a wooden-bodied vehicle of similar build and construction, it's most unlikely that the owner is going to take it apart so you can copy crucial body parts. So the first realistic step in the restoration process is to assess very carefully the condition of each and every piece of the body structure, and then to develop a plan to dismantle those sections that need to be replaced or repaired.

Modern digital camera technology can now play a major role in the deconstruction process, as high-quality lenses coupled with massive amounts of memory space allows the restorer to take literally hundreds of images and from every conceivable angle during the tear-down stage. As if to reinforce the point, Trevor Bradley, who restored a Lea-Francis shooting brake in Scotland, tells us: 'Take as many photographs of the car as you think are needed, then double the number and you will be about halfway there!'

The more thought you put into the dismantling, cataloguing and storing of parts the less hassle you'll have when you try to put the vehicle back together again after rebuilding.

Trevor Bradley advocates using a digital camera to capture every aspect of a vehicle's deconstruction, as it will most certainly help when rebuilding damaged woodwork.

The author's 1936 Ford part way through the strip-down stage.

Many parts will be fragile and will possibly break apart. A good quality foaming glue can be used to bond these parts together again so they can be used for making templates later in the build.

However, it's no good taking images if you don't catalogue them in a way that enables you to find them again easily at a later date. Charles Furman of the San Diego Woodie Club recommends the following strategy: 'Save the images in a computer file folder labelled by the name of the part or the location area – such as "left rear door" or "right rear quarter panel" – which will make finding them later for reference so much easier. This process is very important because it is so easy to forget exactly how things came apart and how they should go back together.'

Jeff Yeagle from Pennsylvania, who is now restoring his fourth woodie, reminds us that most body parts on Ford woodie wagons have Ford part numbers, or will at least be found to correspond to some factory designation somewhere in history. He also stresses the importance of photography:

Photography can play a big part in the restoration process, so I've taken detailed photos of every woodie I have ever encountered, be it complete, disassembled or in any state in between.

Many surviving vehicles, such as my 1940 Ford woodie, show signs of repair. However, comparison with vehicles I've photographed will often provide an insight into what is

TOP: Having plenty of space to dismantle and store parts is also of considerable benefit in any major restoration.

MIDDLE: Make sure you keep every part you take off the car, as they will be perfect for making templates from and as reference material during the rebuilding stage.

BOTTOM: It's a good idea to label parts, either with tie-on tags, tape, or even by writing on the reverse, with details of which area they came from (such as a door) and whether they are from the left or the right side. This could save much confusion at the reassembly stage.

original or accurate, and what is a repair. In addition, vintage or period photos have proved very beneficial. Because woodies were always slightly unusual they drew attention to themselves wherever they went, and old photos can usually be obtained to act as a visual guide as to how the vehicle should be restored.

For instance, when I began the restoration of my 1940 Ford woodie I was able to locate a photo of my car prior to my ownership. From that photo I was able to determine when some repairs to the wooden body were made, and what changes were made and by whom. This proved to be very helpful to determine what was correct and what was incorrect.

ABOVE & TOP: Strip everything off the body until you are left with the bare frame. Depending on the type of vehicle you are deconstructing it may be possible to remove outer panelling or covering to reveal various hidden fixings, but on other vehicles you just won't have that luxury. In either case, it is advisable to strip everything off the body until you are left with a bare frame, before you try to take that apart. This will allow you to inspect every angle and crevice for hidden fixings, and will give you the access you need to remove them.

The roof structure of wood-framed vehicles usually survives remarkably well, often despite the poor condition of the woodwork closer to the ground. Such roof structures were often built as a separate assembly and can often be very heavy, so depending on the condition of the assembly and your own personal restoration requirements, you may choose to leave it in place during the rebuild. Your own circumstances will dictate the best method for you.

However, if your vehicle does have a large roof assembly that you decide to leave in place, you will still probably have to carefully jack it up from the rear of the vehicle to free the top joints that hold the side frame in place.

Many coachbuilders built the roof as a separate unit, and ideally this should be removed to give better access to the side frames. However, it is usually a heavy structure so make sure you have the right lifting equipment or plenty of friends to help you lift it clear of the body.

Apart from camera technology, there is also a use for other forms of modern technology during the deconstruction process. Trevor Bradley used a laser level when he began to dismantle his Lea-Francis, and was glad he did. 'The door posts leaned in by 2in from top to bottom, and that was not at all evident when simply looking at the car. The subtle curving from front to back was also something I recorded, and without that, the car simply wouldn't look right.'

Apart from photographic images, you should also make sketches at every stage and record crucial dimensions – something that you can't do with a camera image. You can also use sketches to record how things move in relation to one another, and also the order in which components come apart.

It is always a good idea to support the body structure with cross bracing (either wood or steel) when removing the roof to ensure the rest of the structure stays in place.

Early Ford woodies used the rear frame of the front bench seat to help tie the B-pillars together. This could be left in place during the early stages of disassembly to ensure the body stays square.

It's also a good idea to label all parts – you can often write details of the part and its location on an inside area that is not going to show. Alternatively, I'll often use a strip of masking tape wrapped around the item with the description written on that.

Perhaps the most important message is that you should never take a rotten body off the frame until you have repaired it, otherwise you'll never get it square or level again and you'll be lucky if you can get the doors to line up or to open and shut properly.

Make sure you label parts with left or right, if appropriate, which could save the hassle of trying to fit a part to the wrong side of the vehicle at the reassembly stage. You could also use coloured tape to identify parts from one area or side, such as, for example, the right rear door or top tailgate.

I have also found it useful to tape together all the parts from one location, such as a door or tailgate, in a bundle, because otherwise small items such as strip mouldings can easily get mixed up. I even go so far as to bag up old screws, washers and mouldings, and attach them to the relevant parts. They can be thrown away at reassembly, but at this stage these old parts can be extremely useful for overcoming undue head scratching.

I've learnt from experience that every coachbuilder assembled their vehicles in their own unique way, and whilst large parts such as doors can normally be removed by unscrewing them from the hinges, taking apart the main assemblies can be somewhat trickier. Many wood-framed vehicles use the roof assembly to tie the structure together and keep it rigid. The roof is often fixed to the side beams by screws and a combination of lap or tenon joints, and the key to successful disassembly is finding how and where these fixings are located.

So if, for example, you or a professional woodworker is going to construct and install completely new bodywork, then removing the roof should be a reasonably straightforward job (though you may need extra help due to its weight). However, if you are going down the partial restoration and repair route, then you should leave the roof in place and work on just one side of the vehicle at a time to retain the structural integrity of the bodywork.

Wooden bodywork can flex and move even when it's in good shape, but once you weaken the structure even further by removing whole sections, then you run the serious risk of allowing it to move out of square. You may not notice an inch or so out of true until you start reassembling the new parts and begin to wonder why the doors don't align properly. Early Ford woodies have a metal structure that forms the back of the front seat, and this screws to both B-pillars and is a perfect mechanism to leave in place to ensure the overall squareness of the bodywork.

I have also found it useful to cut and drill metal plates that can be screwed in place after the door hinges have been removed; I then weld square tubing in the form of an X-brace from these points to ensure the structural integrity of the body whilst it is reduced to a skeleton shell.

STORAGE SPACE

If you have ever attempted to restore a car or van in the confines of a single-vehicle garage, then you'll know how quickly you run out of space not only to store the vehicle and the parts taken off it, but also to physically carry out restoration work.

With a wooden-bodied vehicle you'll end up with a pile of mechanical parts, metal body parts, interior trim, and glass and wooden body parts, and ideally you'll want to store them completely separately. Degreasers, metal filings, and oil and paint from working on the mechanical parts can quickly soil and permanently damage your pristine

wood, while sawdust can wreak havoc with the internal workings of your engine or transmission.

I'm lucky enough to have a fairly large garage and two decent-sized sheds at the bottom of my garden in which I can store parts taken off my woodie away from the stripped down vehicle and out of harm's way. Even better still, I also have an aluminium greenhouse, which is the perfect place to store old timber taken off a vehicle without the risk of any resident bugs, worms or beetles taking up residence in the shed and creating a secondary infestation.

Good housekeeping will ensure that parts don't get lost or broken before you can replace them. Ideally you'll want to build and install shelving before you start work on the tear-down process, and it helps to tag or reference the shelves in such a way that any part can be located when referring to

photographs, drawings and sketches. Upon removal, you know what the part is, where it came from, how you took it off and, hopefully, how it should be replaced. However, six, twelve or twenty-four months down the line, you will probably have forgotten what it is, let alone where it goes.

Have a logical way of referencing the parts. Use logical and obvious terminology, such as front, middle and back – driver's side and passenger side – roof and floor. That way, even if some an item is halfway between top and floor, front and middle, driver's and passenger's side, you know you'll find it eventually!

Lastly, as I've said before, never throw anything away until the vehicle is completely finished. Wrap the parts in plastic if they are rotten or infested with bugs, beetles or worms, but never throw them away until you have made and fitted the replacement.

Dismantling a wooden-framed vehicle for restoration requires a lot of storage space for major body parts. Ron Heiden stores his parts upstairs at his workshop in Southern California.

LEFT: *Body jigs can be stood on their end to minimize storage space, providing your workshop has a high roof.*

I always try to keep metal panelwork well away from the work area and you can minimize the space required by hanging parts from the garage/workshop roof…and don't forget to wrap parts such as the motor in plastic to keep dust and sawdust out!

If you have room to store body parts in a separate building or area well away from the vehicle itself you will minimize the risk of dirt, grease, oil and paint contaminating the wood.

Of course, you could also hang body parts on the wall if you have the space.

If you have to completely strip the car then it might be worth having the steel shell or frame sent off for media blasting or chemical dipping to remove every last piece of rust so that you have a good honest basis to start from.

CHAPTER 5

Stripping Off Old Varnish and Sanding

Unless you are going for a total rebuild using new wood, then you are almost certainly going to have to strip off the layers of old varnish, paint or whatever form of protection had originally been applied to the vehicle, before you can make an assessment of its condition. While there are a number of aggressive methods you might employ to strip paint or varnish off, say, your house or shed, you really need to use much more care when it comes to a vehicle, particularly if the stripped wood is likely to be exposed and viewable on the restored vehicle. In most cases the wood is more likely to be varnished than painted, so for ease of writing style we'll just talk about varnish removal (although the same process would equally apply to paint).

If the varnish is already flaking off the process of stripping might seem easier, but the trade-off could come in the poor condition of the exposed wood underneath. In fact, the better the condition the varnish is in, the better the condition the wood should be in.

Similarly, the better the access to all parts of the wood, the better the result will be. So any glass, plywood or metal panels and doors that can be removed from the frame should be taken out to reveal the bare skeletal frame. The wooden items removed from the frame can be stripped separately later.

Before you start any work on varnish removal make sure you put on a pair of good quality safety glasses, because once you start attacking the old varnish it's all too easy to send pieces of old material flying into your face, no matter what stripping method you employ.

As far as actual stripping is concerned, there are three main processes you can use: hand scraping, using chemical strippers, or sanding. In researching material for this book I have visited a number of professional and home restorers in the USA and the UK and have found that each and every one has their own preferred favourite method. You may well have your preferred method, or it may be that the ideal solution is a combination of these processes. Either way, let's explore all three processes and you can decide which might work best for you.

I've heard of some people using a heat gun to remove old varnish, and while this may work well on your house, where the wood will ultimately be painted over, I've found that it is all too easy to misjudge the amount of heat being generated – heat guns can reach very high temperatures at the nozzle end, making it all too easy to burn yourself, your helper and the

Stripping off the old varnish will reveal the true condition of the wood underneath.

A vehicle that has obviously been neglected and stored for a long time may look sound but you can't tell for sure until you strip off the old varnish.

wood – and a wood burn is permanent and cannot be sanded or bleached out. So for that reason alone I would not recommend their use. Also, heat guns can be exceedingly noisy.

HAND SCRAPING

The simplest way to remove old varnish is by hand scraping, and whilst this process is not for everybody, it is certainly effective. California-based wood guru Ron Heiden is an advocate of removing the varnish from framework using a hand scraper, and when I visited his Leucadia workshops as part of my research for this book, the demonstration he gave made it look very easy.

The main benefit of hand scraping is that it is by far the cleanest and safest method you can use, as there will not be any problems with dust or chemical fumes filling your workshop or garage. It's also probably the cheapest method, as your initial outlay will only involve the purchase of one of the many hand scrapers on the market – Ron's favourite is the long-handled Sandvik scraper with reversible tungsten blades.

The down side, if you can call it that, of using a hand scraper is that the process can be slow and time-consuming and can involve a fair amount of muscle power (although not as much as with hand sanding!). If you read any books or web pages on refinishing fine furniture, you'll see that hand scraping is the preferred method of stripping because it causes the least damage to the wood surface (assuming, of course, that you are not too heavy-handed with the tool).

Scraping by hand is perfect for flat surfaces, and whilst curves, corners and grooves are more of a challenge, they

A good quality, sharp hand-scraping tool is perfect for removing varnish, and you won't have to deal with chemical residue.

Due to the corrosive nature of chemical strippers it is essential to wear good quality protective gloves and eye protectors or goggles.

Chemical stripping is quite straightforward provided you do observe the safety instructions on the side of the can. Most are corrosive and can burn your skin if you don't wear adequate protection – and they can burn plastic, too.

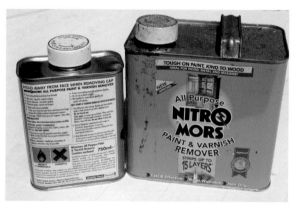

Before using any chemical strippers it is essential to read and digest the safety instructions. Most of these strippers are corrosive, give off toxic vapours and can be flammable, so take extreme care when using them.

Chemical strippers can be highly flammable, so don't use them near any source of heat or naked flame. Also, the cans are prone to pressure build-up in warm weather, so open the cap very slowly to release any pressure so as to avoid any spillage on to your skin or face. Should the worst happen, rinse with water straightaway.

Always decant chemical strippers into either a glass or metal container. However, some such as Nitromors have a handy plastic cover that makes a perfect container, and it is not affected by chemical reaction.

A good quality scraper is all you need to remove the softened varnish once the chemical stripper has done its work.

Most varnishes will need several applications of chemical stripper to remove all traces of old material.

The very last traces of varnish can be removed using a pad of wire wool dipped in chemical stripper.

won't be any more difficult to strip than using either of the other two methods mentioned in this section. Another less obvious benefit of hand scraping is that by using only hand pressure, and by not using any chemicals, you are less likely to break any joints unintentionally.

Using Chemical Strippers

Chemical strippers are something of an antithesis – they do an excellent job, but they are corrosive and make a lot of mess! There will be different products and different brands in various parts of the world, and whilst we will be focusing on a couple of different products in the context of this chapter, I'd urge you to read the specific use and safety instructions that come with whatever product you purchase.

Whatever chemical stripper you do decide to use, you need to remember that such chemicals are highly corrosive, and the agents in them that are capable of softening layers of hard-

ened varnish can burn your skin in no time at all. So safety first.

You will need to wear a pair of good quality rubber or plastic gloves and a pair of protective safety glasses. Long sleeves and long pants or jeans are essential, and if you have long or unruly hair then a hat or cap should be worn. Ideally you will also want a nearby source of clean water, because the slightest speck of chemical stripper or stripped varnish that lands on exposed skin will need to be washed off quickly.

Pressure can build up in cans of chemical stripper, especially if they are left in the sun too long with the cap closed (not recommended). So always remove the cap slowly to release any pressure within, and ideally leave them in a cool place before opening.

Before I apply a chemical stripper I usually start at one end or corner of the vehicle and slowly work my way around it with a small flat-bladed scraper or putty knife purchased from a hardware store. This process will

remove or loosen any large chunks of flaking varnish.

It is also a good idea to think about adjacent bodywork and materials, as any stripped material will contain active chemical agents that will continue to work on any surface they land on. So stripped varnish could still mark or burn any paintwork it lands on – and I know from personal experience, it can also burn into the surface of your shoes!

In the UK, the chemical stripper of choice is 'Nitromors All Purpose Paint & Varnish Remover', which is a dichloromethane-free, fast-acting and highly effective paint and varnish remover. The viscous, semi-gel, non-drip formulation makes it ideal for use on both vertical and horizontal surfaces, giving a thick, even application with deep penetration and prolonged effectiveness. Nitromors advise decanting material into a metal or glass container, although I've found that the green plastic cover that comes with the smaller cans makes a handy container and is not affected by the gel itself.

This stripper is non-acid and non-caustic, but is still very corrosive and gives off toxic fumes. The manufacturer advises that there is a risk of irreversible effect through inhalation, so work on a small area at a time and apply with a brush – preferably in a well-ventilated area – and replace the cap on the can. They also advise not to use the stripper in direct sunlight.

It is highly flammable and so can only be used in a non-smoking environment; it is also very effective at burning into plastic. In fact its manufacturer, Henkel, advises against using it in an environment where there is likely to be any type of spark or static discharge.

If the old varnish is particularly thick then it helps to abrade the surface with sandpaper or wire wool so the chemical can get a stronger 'bite'. That said, I've found Nitromors to be very effective in stripping off thick layers of old varnish and producing a clean and residue-free finish. It has the added advantage that it removes the surface layer of grime in the wood, thus making the cleaning process that much easier.

When all the wood is stripped it should be washed down with a light wash of white spirit and then soapy water and allowed to dry. Failure to do this may result in a chemical residue remaining, which will later affect the adhesion of any stains and varnishes.

If you have a large amount of wood to strip, such as plywood panels and inserts, or maybe a complete roof section, then it will pay to shop around for the best price and buy the biggest can available – possibly a 5ltr or gallon can because you'll need to use a lot of it and although it's expensive, it will cost even more if you buy a number of small cans.

Glenn at Redding Woodworks in Ocala, Florida, is another advocate of chemical varnish strippers, but his product of choice is Klean Strip. This works in a similar fashion to Nitromors in that you pour liquid into a metal container and apply it with a brush. Multiple coats may need to be applied to remove several layers of old varnish, which is scraped off using a plastic stripping tool.

The manufacturers of Klean Strip recommend using a clean surface abrasive pad dipped in 'After Wash' or mineral spirits to loosen any remaining finish and remove any residue.

I am loathe to mention any product, particularly one that is mildly corrosive, without obtaining the full health and safety instructions, and any other tips and advice on usage direct from the manufacturer. However, despite a number of telephone calls to Klean Strip, no such advice was forthcoming – so do please read and digest all the safety information printed on the container before you use it. In fact, that goes for any chemical stripper, wherever you may source it.

SANDING

Whatever method you use to strip off the old varnish you will also end up sanding the wood smooth, which is why many people start off with the sanding process to remove the varnish. Some even do the whole process by hand sanding, but the use of some sort of power tool will undoubtedly make the job so much easier.

When it comes to sanding, the immortal words of Richard McCloskey, 'Sand your wood and then sand some more!' should be ringing in your ears. Rick concurs that disassembling the structure into as many parts as you can will get the best results, and advises:

You need to sand your wood until you have removed all the beat-up, grey, weathered surface layer and you are looking at solid, clean wood. Yes, your car gets slightly smaller every time it is refinished, and you cannot make weather-checking cracks go away!

I start my sanding with 80 grit using a DeWalt random orbital sander to do the dirty work. A 'disc' sander can be very useful here to get at the inside contours and to remove a deeply weathered surface, but, be careful using that disc, it can zip off a lot of your good wood fast!

Continue to machine sand through the grits down to 150 grit before bleaching. Clean up the tight spots by hand-sanding. Remember that after the bleaching process, you will only be able to sand lightly with 220 grit by hand to remove the remnants of grain fuzz lifted by the bleach and its neutralizer. Adequate in-depth sanding preparation of the wood is critical for the bleach to do its work properly.

Using a quality electric sander will undoubtedly speed up the stripping process.

Richard McCloskey advises: 'Sand your wood, then sand it some more.

CHAPTER 6

Selecting the Right Wood

Sourcing the right wood for the construction or restoration of any wooden-bodied vehicle is one of the most fundamental aspects relating to the success or failure of the project. So before you start work you need to identify the type of wood your vehicle was originally constructed from, and then decide if you want to replace it with like for like, or (purists look away now) to use another type of wood.

Wooden vehicle frames were mostly constructed from hardwoods such as ash, oak, maple and beech, some used exotic woods such as mahogany, while some vehicles contained a mixture of woods.

Most coachbuilders had woods they preferred to use, but depending on where the original coachbuilder was based, ultimately the type of wood they used was dictated by their level of expertise, also their access to and the availability and cost of various woods. Whilst there is little to choose between hardwoods in terms of strength, various other properties make some more suitable than others for coachbuilding purposes.

Ash was the wood of choice for British coachbuilders as it was in plentiful supply, but most importantly it has a level of flexibility that allows it to be formed easily into a wide variety

Care sourcing the right type, density and moisture content of the wood you use for your rebuild will be rewarded by the quality of the end result you can achieve.

This UK-bodied 1936 Dodge shows the beautiful grain patterns that ash provides.

Maple was a popular choice for North American coachbuilders, and although the wood has a less intense grain pattern than ash, it more than makes up for this with a gorgeous warm glow when varnished.

Oak is sometimes used for vehicle bodywork but is more commonly used for heavyweight structures such as bus and truck floors.

Thin strips of hardwood glued together to form curved laminations are commonly used in the side members of the 1949–51 Ford 'Shoebox' woodie.

Laminations are also extensively used to form curved structures such as wheel arches, where they can be glued to shape and provide an exceedingly strong structure.

of curves and shapes. It also springs back to its original shape when heavily loaded, and it resists splitting when panel pins are hammered in. Also it has a tight grain, which can give splendid grain patterns on exposed frames if the wood is sawn or cut appropriately.

Whilst some vehicles have been constructed out of oak, the wood is much darker and prone to turning black when in prolonged contact with damp or water. Oak is also slightly acidic and can corrode any metals it comes into contact with – such as the screws holding the frame together!

In addition to solid hardwood frames, some vehicles, such as the 1949–51 'Shoebox' Ford woodies, used some plywood laminate framing. Laminated forms are also used extensively on curved surfaces on coachbuilt cars

where the 'layered edge' is hidden from view by body panels.

Most restorers will remove any plywood panelling and put it to one side whilst they focus on restoring or repairing the vehicle's main hardwood body frame, so it is worth mentioning plywood at this juncture. First, many of the more exotic plywoods that were readily used sixty or seventy years ago with little regard to deforestation or sustainability are now either in very short supply, or no longer available at all. So alternatives may have to be considered at the replacement stage.

Also, it's fair to say that both glue and

wood preservative technology from several decades ago was primitive, if not prehistoric, compared with the chemical marvels that we enjoy today. So whilst factory original plywood panelling on some vehicles delaminated and rotted out in a relatively short time if subject to adverse weather conditions or poor maintenance, it can be replaced with much better quality materials during the restoration process.

SOURCING WOOD

It may sound obvious, but don't assume

Depending on how the timber is sawn, ash can provide some stunning grain patterns, which can really be used to enhance the visual effect of wooden bodywork.

Glues and grades of plywood have advanced significantly in recent years, and materials such as marine-grade plywood should last for decades.

This block of ash further demonstrates the beautiful grain patterns that can be achieved.

ABOVE: Air-dried ash is preferable, but not always easy to come by. Many lumber yards have kiln-dried ash, which typically has a moisture content of between 8 to 12 per cent. However, this can be slightly more brittle – so buyer beware!

LEFT: Ash was the wood of choice for most British woodie wagons, and its superb grain structure is perfect for large upright or horizontal sections.

that whatever wood you are offered is right for the job in hand. After all, you wouldn't walk into a restaurant or a clothes store and say 'Give me any old thing you've got lying around!' So pick your wood carefully, and as woodie legend Ron Heiden suggests, do not buy anything with knots or black spots. Try to obtain the cleanest, straightest timber you can, as 'green' wood will usually bend and end up as a door prop. Ron also advises that with cheap Far Eastern plywood flooding the market, quality has fallen to a level where buying ready-veneered plywood probably won't meet the quality standards we expect for our vehicles; he now veneers his own plywood to ensure constant high quality.

Where and how you source the wood you need for your project will be governed to a large extent by where you live. If you live near a heavily forested area you might be able to acquire your timber locally and let it air dry (season) for a few years in a warm, dry environment, or you may even have access to a kiln-drying facility, which will rapidly speed up the seasoning process. However, most of us will probably end up buying our wood from a timber/lumber yard. Some yards and specialists keep a large stock and have excellent

choice, whilst others will only be fairly limited, so it will pay to shop around, talk to other restorers, and let your fingers do the walking online.

If possible, try to procure timber with a good straight grain that has been dried naturally, as kiln-dried ash is more likely to snap when sawn or put under pressure. The condition is known as 'carroting' in the woodworking world.

White ash is still plentiful, if not exactly cheap. Most British coachbuilders used ash, and a high quality product is now available from the USA: this is denser and of better quality than was originally used, and can be sourced from any number of importers and

suppliers, although the larger stockists are most likely to have a wider selection, which will enable the restorer to obtain consistent grain pattern and colour match.

However, some of the more exotic hardwoods are now becoming difficult to procure due to growing environmental issues over the felling of the rainforest. Although few American woodies survive in the UK today, those that do come up for restoration in the island nation can give restorers a problem, as highlighted by woodie specialist Steve Foreman. He tells us: 'Many American woodies had bodies built from maple, which is not always readily available in

One of the most sought-after types of hard maple is the speckled pattern known as bird's eye. It is often found quite randomly throughout Ford woodies, such as this roof header on the author's 1936 Ford.

the size planks you need. It can also be expensive, so it is essential to check for supplies of the right wood and its cost before you start the tear down.'

It is also essential to ensure you obtain the right grade of wood, as it is not all the same. For instance, maple is often described as 'soft maple' or 'hard maple'. However, the term 'soft maple' does not refer to any specific type of maple, but rather is a broad term that includes several different types of maple: it is used simply to differentiate these species from 'hard maple'.

Hard maple, on the other hand, typically refers to one specific type of maple species: *Acer saccharum*. Hard maple is also known as rock maple or sugar maple (the same tree that is tapped to obtain maple syrup), and in addition to auto framing this is the wood of choice for making baseball bats. Besides this one species of maple, the only other species that is sometimes considered in the grouping of hard maple in the USA is black maple (*Acer nigrum*). Black maple is so closely related to hard maple that some even consider it to be a subspecies of the same tree, classifying it as *Acer saccharum* subsp. *nigrum*.

It goes without saying that 'soft maple' is softer than 'hard maple', which is why it is generally sold at a much lower price than the harder variety. So in the context of sourcing maple for the frame of your vehicle, you should only use the highest quality Hard Rock variety.

As mentioned earlier, where you actually source the wood will depend on where you are located in the world, and whilst few of the sources who contributed to the researching of this book actually named specific suppliers, Glenn Redding from Ocala revealed that he purchases all his lumber from the Heritage Lumber Company in DeLand, Florida. He tells us:

> This company is a wholesale distributor and carries a variety of wood, including plywoods, which makes this part of 'gathering needed materials' quite easy.
>
> All lumber is bought in the rough and must be planed to a desired thickness, depending on the application. All parts are hand made – yes, hand made! The only cutter I own is a finger-jointing machine. Other than standard tools such as a table saw, router and bandsaw, I put in all grooves, curves and so on by hand. Yes, it can be done without special tools, so there is hope for everyone. Just be patient!

CHECKING MOISTURE CONTENT

Wherever you source or buy the wood for your project vehicle, it is essential to make sure that the moisture content is between 8 and 10 per cent. This is usually achieved by either kiln-drying or allowing the wood to naturally air-dry (also known as seasoning) for approximately three to four years. Small hand-held moisture meters are available online or from specialists and are probably a good investment if you have any doubts about the moisture content of the wood you've been offered.

This view is shared by amateur restorer Jeff Yeagle from Pennsylvania, who, after having restored a handful of Ford woodies, knows a thing or two about sourcing the right quality of wood. He tells us:

> Fortunately hard maple, soft maple and ash grow in Pennsylvania, and as a result there are a multitude of outlets where lumber for body construction can be sourced. However, when I select timber I typically carry a lignometer to determine the moisture content. Interestingly, one local sawmill dates each of his pieces of material with date codes, to indicate to customers how long the material has stood.

Wood that has been recently felled or processed, and probably not dried (often referred to as 'green' timber), is liable to have a high moisture content, which can make the wood bend and twist out of shape as it dries naturally. This is not something you'd necessarily notice during the build process (unless of course you spend years working on the bodywork), but as the moisture content decreases with age, then the hardwood frames of doors and tailgates can distort to the point where they no longer close properly. And the remedy could be costly and time-consuming.

In fact one UK restorer told me of some thick planks of ash that he purchased, which had been air-drying for allegedly thirteen years. Yet when he cut out some of the pieces he needed for a truck cab rebuild and ran them through the planer-thicknesser, they warped slightly overnight. So unless you are really sure of the water content of your hardwood I would advise taking your time with the construction.

In fact the moisture content of a piece of timber is something many of us take for granted, says Keith Smith, when writing about the importance of measuring moisture content on getwoodworking.com. He tells us that timber is normally kiln-dried down to about 8 to 10 per cent moisture content, but it will quickly reabsorb moisture if it is stored badly.

Does that matter, he asks. As the moisture content varies, wood expands and contracts, mainly across the grain, so using timber that has not been dried properly is a sure way of ruining a project; in the worst cases the wood can warp and shakes (splits) can appear. Even with a small amount of movement, panels shrink, mitres open up and gaps show at the shoulders of tenons.

How Moisture Can be Measured

Keith reminds us that the moisture content of a piece of timber is measured as a ratio of the weight of the water in the wood relative to its dry weight and is given as a percentage (per cent MC). As it is possible for timber to hold more than its dry weight of water, it can have a moisture content greater than 100 per cent. Timber with a moisture content greater than 20 per cent is open to attack by dry rot spores and is normally regarded as green.

> I have some oak planks stored in the ventilated hayloft over my workshop; some have been air-drying for over ten years while others were kiln-dried, but have spent the last year or so in the loft. Now they all have a similar moisture content, ranging from 16 to 18 per cent, despite the fact it's summer [at the time Keith wrote this]. If I wanted to use this timber for anything other than an outdoor project, I would need to bring it into the house for several weeks. If wood has been dried

A good quality moisture meter comes in useful for checking the moisture content of your wood.

Moisture meters come in a wide range of configurations, but the most useful are those that can just be held against, or placed on, the wood to give a reading.

properly it will soon acclimatize once stored indoors; I usually allow a couple of weeks.

DON'T FORGET THAT PLYWOOD

Most wooden-framed vehicles will contain plywood somewhere in their construction and replacing it also needs careful consideration. Plywood is made up of wafer-thin sheets of wood glued together to form thicker sheets, and these can vary tremendously in content and quality.

Plywood tends to be graded by the type of adhesive used in the bonding process, with three common grades: interior, exterior and marine. The first grade has no place at all on vehicles, and ideally you should use marine grade throughout for the best longevity. One pointer to the quality of grade is the colour of the glue that can be seen at the outside edges.

Industry insiders advise that there is a lot of substandard as well as illegal plywood flooding the market, so they advise doing some basic checks before you part with any money. Poor quality could consist of substandard, rejected and repackaged filler material that may pose health and safety risks. For instance, plywood marked 'for external use only' could well contain high levels of formaldehyde.

Size can also be an issue. Just as supermarket packets get clearly resized downwards so you end up paying more per item, inferior grades of cheap imported plywood can often be thinner than marked, which could throw out your dimensions and fit.

Most major retailers will value their reputation and so probably won't stock inferior quality plywood, and all plywood sold in Europe should carry the CE mark. No CE mark – reject the plywood.

AC guru, Ian Strange, has the following advice:

Ideally you should look for weather and boil proof (WWBP) grade adhesive (or exterior grade) in plywood, but be very careful that you do actually receive exterior grade when ordering. Check that the glue lines between the plies are dark reddish brown – if you can't see any dark glue lines then it's probably interior grade. Birch plywood is best for strength, but note that some birch plywoods only have outer plies of birch, and the rest is made from assorted softwoods.

MAKING PATTERNS

While I'll be looking at pattern making in detail in the following chapter, it is worth mentioning here the wood you'll need to source for pattern and template making – as by now you will have realized that hardwoods, such as ash or maple, will need to be purchased from a specialist and they can be expensive. So, using your prized hardwood for pattern making is not a financially viable option.

Some of you may have the confidence to jump straight in and cut and shape hardwood sections without making any patterns or templates first, but there will be just as many who will have to try to replicate missing sections or even build anew, and I've seen too much nice hardwood reduced to an expensive pile of firewood where restorers have rushed in.

Needless to say, using cheap softwoods such as pine or even plywood to make templates means that you'll be using cheap and readily available materials that won't work out too costly when you dispose of them.

CHAPTER 7

Making Patterns and Templates

Whether you are restoring an existing vehicle or starting from scratch, one of the most important aspects of working on any wooden-framed vehicle body-work is the ability to make patterns or templates from which to work.

Unlike a metal-bodied vehicle where damaged sections can be cut out and repair panels welded, screwed and riveted in, wood does not easily lend itself to being repaired – at least not in a way that produces an invisible repair. In a vehicle where the framework is to be covered over in, say, metal, fabric or plywood panelling, then it may be possible to cut off a damaged section of framework and join a new piece on either by screwing or gluing it.

However, it most cases it will usually be more beneficial in terms of time, visual appeal and cost to shape a new section. Most professionals who have contributed to this book take the view that it is always more cost effective to replace than to repair, and you minimize the risk of disappointment later in the restoration process.

MAKING A PERFECT COPY

As outlined in the earlier section on taking things apart, the importance of careful disassembly cannot be stressed too strongly. Forcing a joint apart or ripping off a piece of rotten timber may destroy tenons and crucially change the shape of components, making them harder to replicate when the time comes.

Making the template as accurate as possible will ensure that the new wood replicates the original in terms of shape and style and, most importantly, fits perfectly. There are a great many ways to make a template, but a lot depends on the condition of the original piece – assuming, of course, that you have an

Whether you are constructing a whole new body frame or just a couple of sections, you'll probably need to make templates and patterns to ensure the size and shape of the new part is a perfect fit.

Full size body side templates can help assess the correct height, shape and lines of any potential body design long before you start cutting that expensive hardwood.

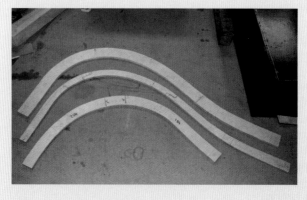

Making templates for even the smallest parts can ensure that you don't waste expensive hardwood cutting a part that doesn't fit.

original piece to work with. (We will examine how to overcome a lack of original parts later in this section.)

The best place to start is before the vehicle is disassembled. Sometimes the old framing will have sagged, so it is important to check the body for squareness before attempting to cut any templates or patterns. If needs be, jack the frame up or use temporary blocks or braces to get it square and level. Then, using sheets of cardboard, you can use pencils or marker pens to outline the shape of major components in two dimensions. Sections that are missing can be loosely drawn in. When these pieces are later removed from the vehicle, the shape of any joints can then be added to the template.

If you have access to a similar vehicle you may be able to make templates from that, assuming that the frame is exposed and accessible.

Chip Kussmaul from Cincinnati Woodworks reminds us that you need to look at the big picture and not just local dimensions when making templates. He advises:

Making templates and patterns of existing parts out of MDF or fibreboard is the perfect way to ensure that you reproduce them accurately. Just be aware of the health and safety issues outlined in Chapter 4.

Make sure you record all horizontal and vertical dimensions. For instance, I make sure that, on the front door, the distance from the lower hinge to the top back corner is the appropriate dimension. If that is right, the rest of the fit-up is easier. If it's wrong, you're screwed.

Also remember that the factory hardware was made with relatively little tolerance. To some extent you have to make your wood fit the hardware, not the other way around.

To sum up, my idea of a useful template is one that has the key points located properly. The best way to come up with such a template is to have access to a similar car. Otherwise try to create a full size template on plywood of the entire side of the car. Determine what are the key points, such as attachment points on the chassis, hinges, brackets and so on. Lay them out as X–Y measurements rather than as part of a pretty picture. Then fill in the shape of the assemblies from there.

HARDBOARD VERSUS PLYWOOD

An alternative to plywood is what is known in the UK as hardboard, which

Factory hardware is often unique to a particular make, model and year so you'll have to make your wood fit the hardware – not the other way around.

is readily available from a wide range of hardware and home maintenance stores in sheets up to 8 × 4ft in size. It is similar to particle board and medium-density fibreboard, but is denser and much stronger and harder because it is made out of exploded wood fibres that have been highly compressed.

Consequently, the density of hardboard is 31lb or more per cubic foot (500kg/m³) and is usually about 50–65lb per cubic foot (800–1,040kg/m³). It differs from particle board in that the bonding of the wood fibres requires no additional materials, although resin is often added. Unlike particle board, it will not split or crack. It is used extensively in the construction industry and furniture trade. Hardboard is produced in either a wet or dry process: the wet process leaves only one smooth side,

while the dry-processed hardboard is smooth on both sides.

One of the great things about hardboard is that it is flexible, easy to cut and relatively durable, which is why it is popular in the furniture industry for those out-of-sight panels such as the backs of cabinets and wardrobes. Steve Foreman of Forwoodies is an advocate of hardboard templates and adds:

I find it particularly useful for taking full-size shapes and dimensions from a vehicle while the wood frame is still in place, thus providing lines, shapes and dimensions. If the vehicle's woodwork is in poor shape it is better to make the templates while the body is in one piece and before it disintegrates whilst being disassembled.

It is also a good idea to take patterns of individual panels and doors, as they can be offered up during the rebuild to check dimensions and fit. If the wood is off the car and bits are missing then lay the sections on to a sheet of hardboard and draw the overall shape required; that way if bits are missing you can easily fill in the gaps. Having got a one-dimensional plan, a second set of patterns will need to be made for any sections with a double curve.

These hardboard patterns are there so that you can cut the right size and shape of a replacement section – they don't need to have much detail. So if you are replacing a rear pillar you want two pieces of hardboard enabling you to cut a double curve of the right dimensions. All the rebating and jointing can be worked out later, but it is important to start off with the right-sized lump of wood. Most of this is probably stating the obvious, but maybe it will offer some help.

A CLEAR SOLUTION

One of the great things about asking so many professionals and amateurs to give their views on what works for them is that you always get some really valuable input. Whether it will be right for you is only for you to know, but Jeff Yeagle came up with a real gem when he suggested using Plexiglas for making templates. Plexiglas is a thermoplastic and transparent plastic (chemically, it is the synthetic polymer of methyl methacrylate, for those who wish to know such things) and is sold under a variety of trade names; it is not to be confused with Lexan, which is far more rigid and impact-resistant. Jeff tells us:

I have often used Plexiglas, or similar, from which to create templates. The clear nature of the product allows the user to check the fit of patterns visually not only on the original part (from which the pattern is developed), but also to verify that the new part fits precisely to the profile of the original.

Several years ago I designed and manufactured a crude but effective router duplicator based on commercially available designs that I had seen others utilize. The process of its use was best described as monotonous and tiring (which those who utilize commercially available duplicators confirm is a common theme). Recently I have begun to create CAD drawings of various parts, including a drawing of the C pillar for my 1948 Olds woodie, and mirrored the part in Autodesk Auto-CAD to create a missing piece of my own puzzle.

Given the two options I would make a blanket statement that both processes take about the same amount of time (that of creating engineering drawings to scale, and manually recreating an object with a duplicator), and if only one part were ever to be created, certainly the latter is the more effective method of manufacture. However, someone with access to CNC will surely benefit from the modelling of a part and the manufacture using this process.

MAKING TEMPLATES FROM OLD OR MISSING WOOD

So how do you go about making templates for new parts from old, rotten and missing wood? If we are replacing single pieces in a project where most of the wood is sound, we need to blend

ABOVE LEFT: Templates can be used to transfer shape and dimensions on to new wood.

ABOVE RIGHT: Hardboard or MDF templates can be tacked directly on to the wood section and used as a guide for a router wheel to run against, thus making a perfect copy.

BOTTOM LEFT: Hardboard templates are easy to make and provide a permanent reference to the shape and dimensions of individual wooden pieces

the wood into the existing structure and so have to allow for any shrinkage resulting from wet rot, dry rot and wasting. Thus once the wooden item is off the vehicle you must allow for such shrinkage – and then some, before cutting begins.

Trevor Bradley advises that if you are tackling the replacement of a complete door, or even the whole wooden body, then you must take a logical approach to the order in which the parts are fabricated:

> Doorposts and roof rails must go in first. Having one of the old doors is less likely to be of use in these circumstances, because even with the best will and the best tools in the world, you will end up with slightly different dimensions 'between the posts'. You can then use the old wood as a gauge to see how much bigger or smaller the new wooden parts should be.
>
> Adding thickness and length to rotten wooden members will depend on how much the old wood has been attacked. Shrinkage will occur naturally once rot has dried out, but in some cases you may need to 'bridge the gap'.

Rotten, crumbling and missing wood is the hardest to make templates from, but the more photographs and measurements you can take, as well as making formers to duplicate angles and curves, then the better the replacement structure will look.

It may be possible to coat the old wood with a wood hardener compound or liquid to help it retain some element of structural integrity whilst being disassembled, but making a template first will guarantee the new piece will retain the shape of the original.

CHAPTER 8

Dealing with Bugs and Making Repairs

In simple terms, the restoration of wooden-framed automotive bodywork need not necessarily involve fabricating and building a completely new body. Cost, personal taste or the wish to retain something of the original patina can all be deciding factors, but unless you are dragging some termite-infested pile of kindling out of the hedge, then there are probably body parts that will be reusable.

Another major deciding factor in the repair versus total replacement argument will be whether the damaged wooden structure will be visible on the restored vehicle or perhaps covered in some sort of panelling. On a wooden-framed shooting brake/station wagon, where the complete structure is exposed, repairs will take skill and effort to blend in without being glaringly obvious. However, on a vehicle where the frame is covered by panelling, maybe on both the exterior and interior, the strength of the repair can take precedence over visual appeal.

DEALING WITH BUGS

Most repairs will be necessitated by the loss of structural integrity caused either by water ingress, or some form of wood-munching bugs. Whilst rotten wood can be safely put aside to be replicated at a later date, any form of bug infestation needs to be treated like a contagious disease and treated with respect until you are sure it has been eradicated. After all, you'd be hardly likely to invite a person carrying

Woodworm has completely ravaged the waist rail on this door. With such damage a repair would be almost impossible to complete successfully, so replacement would be the best option.

Woodworm holes could be plugged with hardwood dowling, but with so many on a highly visible waist rail on a door you would probably achieve a more desirable result by replacing the complete section.

Decay on this level can only be remedied by replacement.

Seemingly minor damage as seen here on the edge of the running board and the main wooden chassis cladding would be time-consuming to repair as the work involved could necessitate dismantling the whole structure to remove the damaged parts.

 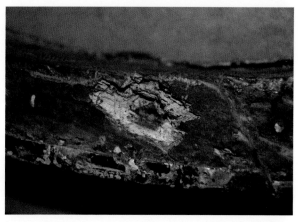

These two shots show the bug damage that could be lurking behind a seemingly strong metal corner section. However, with the wood decaying from the inside out, the frame has lost its structural integrity.

a contagious deadly disease into your home to share a meal. In the same way, transporting a disease-ridden hulk of a vehicle from its resting place on top of a termite mound and placing it inside your timber-framed garage is just asking for trouble. The worst case scenario is that the bugs could then infest your house.

In an ideal world you'd take that bug-infested vehicle and place it inside a meat storage freezer at 15° below (Fahrenheit or Celsius) for twenty-four hours and freeze the creatures solid before dragging it home. However, in the real world you'll have to approach the problem on a smaller scale.

Clearly there are different bugs in different parts of the world, but generally there are those that lay eggs (to do damage later) and fly away, and there are those that take up residence.

Woodworm

Powder post beetles in the USA (generally the same as woodworm in the UK) are more predominant in some regions than others. Glenn Redding, of Florida-based Redding Woodworks, tells us that he finds it very hard to totally eradicate them as they lie dormant for ages, often only to re-emerge after the vehicle is fully restored.

I can certainly vouch for the validity of this statement, having recently found a couple of new woodworm holes in my newly restored 1936 Ford woodie after it emerged from its winter hibernation in the UK. One of the problems with woodworm is that inside the framework of the car the grubs bore a network of tiny tunnels of a complex-

ity that would rival the underground (subway) railway system in London: not only does this weaken the structure, but it is sometimes hard to find every single track and outlet, as there may literally be hundreds.

Generally you only see woodworm holes when the grub has turned into a small moth and literally flown the nest, but assuming you intend to retain that section of wood (we'll talk about repairing it later) you first need to try, and I repeat try, to ensure that you can make it as bug free as possible.

In the UK there are various brushable treatments available for woodworm, as well as pressurized systems that enable you to inject treatment directly into the bore holes – and this is generally where you find it squirting back out of fifty holes you didn't even know existed, and some up to a foot or so from the initial injection point!

Glenn Redding advises that injecting epoxy resin into bore holes not only helps to eradicate any bugs still in residence, but most importantly will help build strength back into the wood. Glenn sensibly burns all old infested wood once patterns have been made.

Termites

Unlike woodworm or similar boring bugs, termites tend to take up permanent residence. Some say that if you stop and listen next to a heavily infested vehicle you can actually hear the sound of the wood being eaten from the inside out. Furthermore, generally once bugs have turned an old vehicle into a 'termite taxi' you will almost certainly be going down the replacement

road rather than trying to repair the wood, as it will prove almost impossible to put structural integrity back into it. However, Glenn recalls finding a most unusual way to eradicate termites, and this was virtually by accident.

A customer's station wagon was trailered to my workshops, but as it had an obvious termite colony on board we decided to park the trailer in a paddock some distance from the buildings whilst we planned its rebuild. The very next day I noticed that fire ants were swarming on the trailer, and within hours the car was covered in ants. The aggressive ants swarmed the car for about three days – and then they left, as quickly as they had appeared. The end result was no termites – job done – thanks, ants!

However, most of us won't have access to a 'friendly' fire-ant colony to do our dirty work and will have to face the problem in a different way. In fact a vehicle that looks halfway decent and seems to be an easy restoration project could easily end up requiring a whole new body if termite damage is found to be significant. Most people who have had any involvement with termites will tell you that it is often a slow and time-consuming process to get rid of them.

If you live in an area where termites are not normally found you might find it difficult to locate a pest-control expert to give you advice or help with the problem – but if you do go down that route, try to find an expert who offers chemical-free fumigation as it is better for the environment. In the USA, the FDA will not allow an individual to acquire and/or use the fumigation chemicals used by experts, so a major infestation is going to be difficult to control without expert help.

However, if you can remove the infested parts from the structure these can be bagged up together with poison pellets, or they could be placed in a freezer for at least two weeks: this will ensure that both bugs and eggs are killed. Once the parts have been removed from the freezer, you will need to leave them inside the bags for a further two days to ensure no condensation forms on the wood, which could later cause mould problems.

REPAIRING THE DAMAGE

Having destroyed the bugs, let us now look at the damage caused, and consider the ongoing debate of whether to repair or simply replace the part. Glenn Redding succinctly sums up the issue thus: 'You need to consider how the vehicle will be used, and what region it will be used in. Most customers want repairs to match old wood, but some don't.' And his views are compounded by Morris Minor Traveller expert Steve Foreman, who states:'Everything has to match or it just won't look right...I won't let in small repair pieces as they eventually shrink, leaving a gap.'

Bug Hole Repairs

One of the problems facing restorers when tackling bug hole repairs is often that the structure can be in great shape apart from a few ugly holes, and there's a temptation to try filling the holes with varnish or some off-the-shelf wood filler and hope that nobody will notice. But believe you me, they will… Varnish doesn't work (I know – I've tried) and wood fillers are meant to be painted over and not stained and/or varnished, as they have a nasty habit of turning bright yellow, thus giving your prized vehicle the impression that it has developed a rash.

Having found a few sections with bug holes during the restoration of my 1936 Ford, I sought professional advice and found the ideal solution at Clanfield Coachbuilding, run by Peter Baylis. Peter showed me how he had dealt with a similar problem on a customer's 1937 Ford woodie, and until I saw the 'before' photos I wouldn't have believed that the car had ever suffered a bug problem in the first place. Peter's solution was simple yet very effective, and I will describe how I used it to good effect on my car.

The first thing is to source a supply of 2mm hardwood dowelling from a model shop. I found such a shop in Windsor, and it stocked specialist hardwood supplies for people building scale-model wooden boats; so I was able to purchase a number of metre lengths of 2mm hardwood dowelling.

It is important to stress the use of hardwood dowelling, as not only is it obviously stronger than softwood, but it has a tighter grain pattern that will absorb stain (and we'll come to that a little later) in the same way as the wood it is being inserted into. I know

The porcupine effect: insert and glue 2mm hardwood dowelling into every single woodworm hole.

Once the glue has dried you can then cut the dowelling flush with the frame and prepare for sanding flush.

Once the frame is re-stained the dowelling may be slightly darker than the surrounding surface, but it won't take on the lurid hue normally associated with wood fillers.

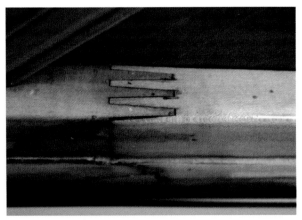

Despite your best efforts you may not totally eradicate bugs at the first attempt. If you look closely you'll see a couple of 'fresh' holes on the left of the finger joint – compare them with the 'dowelled' holes over on the right.

of restorers who have used toothpicks instead of dowelling, but I wouldn't recommend this practice because toothpicks are made from rubbish wood and won't stain correctly.

Before commencing with the repair it is essential that the frame to be repaired is stripped of all varnish and is in a state ready to be resanded and stained, as appropriate. So, assuming you have acquired your supply of 2mm dowelling, you then drill every single bug hole to a depth of approximately 10mm using a 2mm drill bit. The reason for using this size drill is that woodworm manage, very conveniently, to make their bore holes virtually this size so the drill is barely touching the sides.

So, with holes drilled, dip the end of the dowelling in adhesive of your choice – I used regular PVA – and insert it tightly into the hole. It's usually dry in about ten minutes, at which time you can slice the dowelling flush with the frame using a sharp knife, modelling knife or scalpel, and move on to the next hole(s). It is rare to find just one or two holes, and you'll probably find a great many once you start, but

You would have to look hard to see that the end of this interior garnish moulding has had new wood spliced in, restained and varnished.

ABOVE: How you splice in new wood to main structural sections will depend on whether the piece will eventually be panelled over, or varnished and left visible. You clearly wouldn't want exposed screw heads showing on a woodie station wagon, for instance, but otherwise this is a good quality repair.

all the hard work will be worth it in the end.

Once you have filled every hole, sand the frame smooth and inspect the result. If you've previously stained the wood then I would recommend washing the surface with a diluted stain solution and see how that dries. If you are using a water-based stain you can apply it using a damp rag. You may find that the dowelling dries slightly darker than the surrounding wood, but that's surely much better than the bright yellow spots you'll get using wood filler.

Splicing and Dicing

This curved section would originally have been made in sections, so there is no problem in splicing in the sound front section.

Dealing with damaged or rotten wood is, thankfully, much easier than dealing with bug damage. If the damage is in a section that will be hidden from view once the body is repanelled, then you could possibly splice in a new section, shaped using a template. The new section is spliced on the angle to maximize the size of the joining area and can be sanded as appropriate.

On areas where the spliced section is exposed, careful matching of grain, and possibly staining and varnishing, can help to make the join blend in perfectly and become almost invisible (there is more on this technique in Chapter 15). On a vehicle such as a woodie where it may be desirable to keep as much of the original wood as possible, a wafer-thin veneer-like slice of appropriate wood may be glued over the join, thus hiding the spliced repair almost completely.

It can be clamped in place to check the positioning before gluing and screwing.

On a visible interior section it is crucial to splice in new wood that has a grain pattern similar to the original.

New body moulding blends perfectly with the older sound wood.

This Rolls-Royce Phaeton has had new wood skilfully blended with sound original wood.

All woodworm holes should be blasted with an appropriate spray, which is when you find out how extensive the network of bore holes really is.

CHAPTER 9

Bleaching and Preserving

Like any organic material, wood absorbs dirt, grime and particles from the atmosphere over the years. It can also be affected by dampness and water ingress, and will eventually become discoloured, stained and blotchy in appearance.

While varnish strippers and sanding will remove a percentage of surface discoloration, the only effective way of removing dirt that is embedded below the surface is with a process known as wood bleaching. Bleaching is accomplished by using one or a combination of chemical processes designed specifically for wood.

WOOD BLEACHING

Remember that whatever bleach you use, the results will be permanent – you

Wooden-bodied station wagons were high-maintenance vehicles in that the exposed woodwork had to be re-varnished every few years to keep the wood protected from the elements. Failure to do so meant that the varnish would flake off allowing the wood to discolour and in some cases turn almost grey.

Wood this discoloured will need bleaching to bring the natural 'brightness' back to the wood.

Sanding will only remove a proportion of surface dirt and grime.

may be able to re-stain if you make the wood too light, but uneven bleaching is very hard to remedy. Make sure the wood is absolutely clean, and touch it as little as possible to allow the bleach to penetrate the wood evenly.

Before applying the bleach, test it on a scrap piece of the same wood or on a hidden part of the vehicle structure. This will enable you to understand exactly how bleach will react with your wood and how fast that reaction will be. As a general rule, bleaches act quickly on softwoods and slowly on hardwoods.

Bleaching isn't difficult, but it does require some precautions – bleaches are fairly strong chemicals. The stronger ones can damage skin, eyes and lungs (and also your garments), so always wear rubber gloves and safety goggles when working with bleach, and make sure your working area is well ventilated. Follow the bleach manufacturer's instructions exactly. If you get bleach on your skin, wash it off immediately.

Bleaching also requires careful application and removal. With any bleach, use a synthetic bristle or a nylon brush – the chemicals will damage natural bristles. Apply the bleach along the grain of the wood, wetting the surface evenly and thoroughly – there should be no dry spots and no puddles.

After bleaching, wipe the wood clean with a damp cloth. To remove any residue, neutralize the wood thoroughly; use an ammonia solution for oxalic acid and a borax solution for laundry bleach or two-part bleaches.

Wash the bleached wood thoroughly with the appropriate neutralizer; be careful not to overwet it. Then, working quickly to prevent water damage, rinse the wood with clean water and dry it thoroughly with a soft cloth. Let it dry for at least two days before doing any further work on it.

Laundry Bleach

Laundry bleach is often overlooked by

those restoring a wood-framed vehicle in their search for a 'specialized' product. It's certainly not the strongest bleaching agent, but it is cheap and easy to use, and it could be the ideal product to start with. As with all bleaching agents, try it on a test piece of wood first – perhaps the back of a piece of the vehicle frame to gauge the speed of any reaction. Once you are happy with the result you can apply chlorine laundry bleach at full strength to the wood, brushing it evenly over the entire surface.

If you are removing spots or lightening discoloured areas, apply bleach at full strength to those areas. Laundry bleach works quickly: after a minute or two, you should be able to see the stain fading. If you are bleaching out an old stain, wipe the bleach off with a damp cloth when the stain has lightened.

If you are spot bleaching to remove small spots or to blend colour areas, wait until the bleached spots are roughly the same colour as the rest of the wood, then apply bleach again over the entire surface. Remove the bleach with a damp cloth when the colour is even.

Finally, neutralize the treated wood with a solution of one cup of borax dissolved in 1 quart (approximately 1 litre) of hot water. Neutralize, rinse with clean water and dry it thoroughly.

Oxalic Acid

Oxalic acid is available from some hardware stores and wood speciality shops, and from catalogues and online stores. It comes in crystals that are mixed with warm water and applied with a brush or sponge. Minor wood discolorations are a good candidate for this chemical, but it is not really effective at removing major dark areas on hardwoods. It is the active ingredient in most 'deck washes'.

Oxalic acid is not caustic, but it is poisonous. Wear rubber gloves and safety goggles, and make sure that ventilation is adequate. To prepare the acid, mix a saturated solution with warm water, following the instructions on the container. Make sure you prepare enough acid to treat the entire surface.

Apply the acid solution evenly to the wood, brushing it on along the grain to cover the whole surface. Let the acid

Eye and skin protection is essential when working with any types of bleach.

work for about twenty minutes, then wipe it off with a damp cloth. If the surface isn't fully or evenly bleached, reapply the acid as necessary. It's a good idea to buy a pack of really cheap brushes for this task, as each one used in wood bleach will dissolve fairly quickly.

On hardwoods, complete bleaching may take up to an hour. Wipe the wood clean with a damp cloth and wash it with clean water. Then neutralize it with a solution of one cup of household ammonia and 2 quarts (approximately 2 litres) of water. Rinse it again with clean water and dry it thoroughly.

Two-Part Bleaches

The two components of the bleach – labelled '1' and '2' or 'A' and 'B' – are sometimes applied by mixing equal quantities, or sometimes applied separately. Read the manufacturer's instructions and follow them exactly. If applied separately, the first solution is usually allowed to work for about twenty minutes before the second solution is applied.

Following the directions carefully, apply the first solution and let it work; then apply the second solution. One treatment usually bleaches the wood completely, but if the wood isn't light enough, treat it again. Wipe the bleached wood clean with a damp cloth, and then neutralize it with a solution of one cup of borax dissolved in 1 quart (approximately 1 litre) of hot water. Rinse the wood with clean water and dry it thoroughly.

Seasoned professional restorer Rick Mack, who specializes in 1949–51 Fords and Mercury station wagons at his Lakewood, Washington, workshop, has some strong words of advice for those contemplating using two-part wood bleaches:

While the results may be the same, each available brand has slightly different instructions, so please read them very carefully.

I now prefer to use 'DALYS' brand, which can be applied either in a mixed 'A' and 'B' solution, or the 'A' solution can be applied first, followed by the 'B' solution. This flexibility of application is very convenient. In the past I used 'Nu-Tone' brand quite successfully, but I have not found it to be available in the north-west USA. I would suggest trying a small test piece first as some

alternative brands can leave a crusty residue that is most difficult to remove. Please read the instructions carefully on whichever brand you choose!

I cannot emphasize caution enough! These solutions are both hot and caustic, especially the 'B' solution – they will make toast of whatever they touch except wood!

Always use rubber or plastic gloves, and wear splash glasses, and don't spill the stuff on your paint, on your clothes or on your skin! It will not kill if you get some on your hands, but when you see your fingertips turning white they will start to burn like crazy! If you do spill some on your skin, rinse the part thoroughly with water for a couple of minutes, and you'll be fine.

Virtually all of these 'A and B' two-part bleaches require a 'neutralizer' such as plain water, water mixed with white vinegar, or some secret concoction that they sell you along with the bleach. Water always works as a neutralizer in a pinch! The same neutralizer step is also necessary when using the oxalic acid type wood bleach. Again, consult the specific instructions that come along with the bleach that you have purchased.

ABOVE: Two-part bleach is easy to use, and usually works very quickly. The two parts can be applied separately, or mixed together, depending on which brand you buy.

RIGHT: If applied separately, brush the first part well into the grain and allow it to work for approximately twenty minutes.

While Part A helps to soften any ingrained dirt and stains, Part B is corrosive so expect an almost immediate reaction when it is applied. Also, make sure that any areas not being bleached are covered up as bleach spots can affect surrounding wood and paintwork.

Part B needs around two hours to work its magic, so please be patient!

While stained or discoloured wood will obviously need bleaching, any wood that has been exposed to the elements without varnish for more than a few weeks should ideally be bleached during the refinishing process. As the majority of the vehicle types owned by readers of this book will probably have been around for a few decades, the chances are that little original varnish now remains on those vehicles. Therefore bleaching is going to be necessary for almost everyone who is restoring a wood-framed vehicle today, and if carried out correctly will certainly improve the quality of the finished project.

Without bleaching, many areas of the wood will appear far darker and unevenly toned after varnishing. This effect may not appear to be a problem when looking at wood that has been carefully stripped of its old varnish and sanded smooth, but this same wood will most likely appear quite different after the application of new varnish. Rick Mack can speak from experience:

When restoring my first woodie, a 1940 Ford with decent wood, I learned about bleaching only after all sixteen beautiful coats of varnish had been successfully applied.

How come this wood is still so dark after all of that sanding, I asked myself, and I wonder what that stuff on the hardware store shelf labelled wood bleach is? It was definitely a learning experience, and it took two more total refinishings to get it right!

If you are using 'A' and 'B' bleach, pour 10 or 12oz of 'A' into a plastic glass or porcelain container (never use metal) and, using the cheap nylon brush, begin applying the bleach to the wood. It is best to start with a piece or two of trim that you can control while you get used to the feel of applying the solution.

Work quickly and evenly with no drips on the rest of the wood, as it will cause bleached spots which may not even out in tone later! Any missed spots will be darker, perhaps forever. Be thorough! Wet all sides and surfaces,

back and front; get everything with the bleach.

After the wood is completely wet with bleach, take a rag and wipe off the excess, leaving no pools or puddles in the corners and crevices. Let it dry to at least damp, with some brands 'dry'. As the 'A' solution dries, the wood will actually grow darker! Now pour 10 or 12oz of 'B' into a different cup and, using a separate cheap brush, do the whole works all over again, being very careful to cover every bit of wood that was originally coated with the 'A' solution.

Remember to use the rubber gloves! The 'B' solution is the hot one! When the 'B' solution has been completely applied, wipe off the excess again with a clean rag or heavy paper towel. Set the wood out in the sun to bleach and dry – bleach works much more thoroughly in the sun! Cool, huh?

When the bleached wood has dried completely it should be several shades lighter. Now is the time to apply the appropriate neutralizer. Read the

After the bleach has been neutralized and cleaned, the wood will be noticeably lighter. You may need to re-bleach to get the effect you desire, but be careful, as over-bleaching can virtually remove the grain.

After a light sanding the bleached area is noticeably lighter.

instructions on your brand of bleach and follow them. After the neutralizer is dry, check out the wood: does it look satisfactory? Is it light enough? Sometimes a second application of the bleach is necessary. If you think the wood needs it, do it.

Perform the above procedure to all the wood you wish to bleach. It is best to bleach all your wood so it will all be the same tone when your work is finished. You might even consider bleaching the inside wood as well, because bleaching really brightens up the appearance of the finished wood.

I sometimes find it necessary to bleach the new wood replacement pieces too, so that the overall tone is uniform between old and new wood. Before applying the varnish, I do attend to replacing the warm wood patina/tone that the wood bleach removes during the bleaching process.

Some of the potential problems you may encounter include uneven bleaching, missed areas, and loss of the original, warm wood patina. A few slightly off-colour streaks almost always appear somewhere. I have never been able to figure out why this occurs, but a great way to get a final even tone is to utilize the oxalic acid bleach for a final coat in this process.

So, get some of this bleach and mix it and apply to all wood that has been bleached with the A and B-type bleach. Set the wood out in the sun again, and let it dry and neutralize. When finally dry, the wood should be very light in tone, and with a feather-light hand-sanding with 220 grit it will be ready for a new finish!

PRESERVING THE WOOD

As a general rule, the vehicles that we restore today probably had non-existent levels of wood preservative applied when they were built. Not only was the technology of chemical preservatives in its infancy back in the 1930s, 1940s and 1950s, but to be honest, vehicle manufacturers and body builders were in the business of making money, and this usually meant knocking out finished products as fast as they could. So who really cared if the thing fell apart after ten or fifteen years?

So whilst there are now some technically advanced wood preservatives on

Cuprinol is a popular brand of wood preservative in the UK. Here we see it being brushed on to larch floorboards that will form the base of a restored bus.

the market, many restorers will argue that their vehicles will now lead such a pampered life that their precious wood is hardly likely ever to get wet, so such preservatives are hardly necessary. However, although the use of epoxy sealants and high quality marine-grade varnish is most likely to keep out everything that Mother Nature can throw at it, I still believe that the use of preservatives has a place in the rebuild and construction stage.

The seasonal damp climate suffered in the UK has led to the development of some excellent wood preservatives to help counter the problem of terminal wood decay. There are even products that can be used to help extend the life of fairly rotten timber, but they don't have a place on our vehicles, or in this book.

I personally have had excellent results using Cuprinol, which is a general purpose preserver for the protection of sound wood against rot, decay, mould and staining fungi. It is suitable for use on all sound timbers, including structural timbers and joinery. It can be painted, stained, varnished or polished when dry, and will not affect the ultimate colour of the wood.

It can be brushed on to bare wood straight from the can (two to three coats are recommended), and as it has the consistency of water, it flows on quickly and easily. Recoat before the previous coat is dry. Whilst wet, it darkens the wood so you can easily see where you have applied it, and any areas that you may have missed.

However, when dry the wood reverts back to its natural colour. It should be noted that Cuprinol should not be thinned.

I've heard of restorers using a length of plastic guttering (with both ends capped) to make an effective bath for wood preserver whereby smaller items can be totally immersed (for a period of between ten to sixty minutes), thus allowing the preserver to soak right into the grain of the wood. Drying is slow and dependent on temperature and humidity, and it can take between one and five days under average temperatures with good ventilation; it will take longer under less favourable conditions.

To ensure maximum protection of individual strips, these can be immersed in wood preserver for 30min, which should give it enough time to soak right in. A length of plastic drainpipe (with the ends sealed, of course) can be used as the perfect wood bath.

CHAPTER 10

How to Build Wood-Framed Bodywork – an Introduction

Having looked at all the stages that prepare for, and lead up to, actually building new bodywork, you should now be on the downward path to completion. The following four chapters describe the build processes involved in specific bodywork types, but before we delve into these, let's quickly touch on some general issues that will be faced on all types of wood-framed bodywork. For the record, where individuals recommend specific products it is important to bear in mind that these products may not be available in your region or country, and also that inclusion in this book is in no way a recommendation to use these products: it is simply information on what specific individuals have found works best for them. So

on that basis, you have to rely on your own judgement and apply the necessary caution and common sense when using such products.

GLUE VERSUS SCREW

When coachbuilders first assembled the vehicles we restore today, back in the 1930s, 1940s and 1950s, they were built as part of a commercial enterprise that existed to make a profit. So they were built to perform a function and look good when they left the factory, with scant regard for their longevity or possible restoration in the future.

Animal glues were commonly used along with regular steel screws, both of which resulted in problems in later

life. Woodworm and wood-boring beetles are attracted to these old-style glues, and will often turn the tenons that were supposedly holding a joint together into mush. I once purchased a set of four woodie doors that looked, and felt, structurally sound until I tried to work on them and they literally 'exploded' into individual pieces because the joints were nothing more than bug-addled honeycomb!

Many of the experts consulted in the research for this book pointed out that much of the decay and/or bug damage on wood framing is generally located around the joints. Whether this is down to the poor quality of original glues or jointing techniques, which over the years have allowed penetration by

Building wood-framed bodywork need not be a daunting task, providing you are methodical and follow the processes outlined in the following chapters.

TOP: There were a great many 'period' bodges carried out when wood-framed vehicles were still quite numerous on the roads. Metal corner brackets were popular, but perhaps the most ingenious was the use of a thread steel bar running horizontally to hold the structure together once the joints had rotted out.

BELOW: While animal glues were popular in the 1920s, 1930s and 1940s, modern adhesives are helping to make joints much stronger and more waterproof.

LEFT: Modern adhesives are stronger and easier to use than 'old school' glues.

RIGHT: 'Foaming' adhesives are great for gluing together pieces where the surfaces may not be completely flat.

'Foaming' adhesives are immensely strong, and the foam can be scraped off in areas where it is not needed as a fill material.

Screws are used to secure joints while the glue sets. These joints and screws will be hidden once an outer aluminium skin is applied.

either water or bugs or both, is open to conjecture. However, you can do much to eradicate this problem in the future.

Steel screws may have been quick, easy and cheap to install in a factory or workshop back in the old days, but they can be a nightmare to tackle in the twenty-first century when fifty-plus years of decay have turned the heads into rust flakes. However, as a general rule, the fact that the original body builders used screws will usually allow disassembly today without having to use a sledgehammer.

One advocate of screwing the joints is home woodie restorer Ian Brown, who reminds us to consider the philosophy followed by piano ('pianola') restorers – always assume someone will be working on this artefact in the future. This view is supported by coachbuilders at the heavier end of the vehicle market,

such as those restoring truck cabs and bus bodies. Moving forwards, we have the ongoing debate of how we should secure the joints on our rebuilt or new-build bodywork.

I must admit to previously being an advocate of just screwing the joints with no additional glue after a bad experience with super-strength wood glue, when removing a damaged ply-wood panel resulted in the panel coming away from the car together with a huge chunk of the hardwood frame bonded to it. Nevertheless, the virtually universal view of both amateur and professional restorers who took part in my research is that modern glues provide levels of strength and protection that screws simply won't provide on their own.

Ian Strange, who specializes in restoring coachbuilt AC 2-litre saloons in the

UK, reminds us that the main reason for wooden frames rotting out in the first place was water ingress in the joints, and that as well as additional strength, modern waterproof adhesives should provide water protection that should stop joints rotting out in the future. Ian tells us:

In the UK, coachbuilders seem to have increasingly gone over to screwing and gluing virtually all frame joints. I advocate gluing and screwing these joints during restoration because glue adds strength and stiffness to the joint. However, I strongly recommend that any form of animal glue is not used, even for the sake of originality – let's face it, when a car rots away it will end up less original anyway.

Most PVA adhesives (although there are various types) are also not suitable. I have found that the ideal adhesive is the liquid phenol-resorcinol adhesive, which is a two-part resin and hardener. This type of adhesive is often recommended – it is used for boats and gliders, and the brand is still commonly known as Aerodux (as produced by Cyber Geigy in the past).

Aerodux 185 is now part of the Prefere range of adhesives produced by Dynea. It has cold-setting, weather-proofing and gap-filling properties that are especially suited for use in exterior structural components. When fully cured, the manufacturers claim it is resistant to acids, weak alkalis, solvents and even boiling water, and in addition to its use on wood it is also suitable for bonding a wide range of materials to porous substrates.

This complicated section, which helps secure the base of the windscreen pillar to the bulkhead/ firewall on a coachbuilt saloon, is actually made from two pieces spliced together. This would definitely benefit from the use of modern adhesives to secure it firmly in place.

Chip Kussmaul, from Cincinnati Woodworks, tells us: 'I epoxy all joints. There is absolutely nothing stronger. A screw is only holding at the threads, whereas glue is holding along the entire surface.'

Ian concludes: 'Whilst flexing is desirable, too much flexing may lead to cracked panels and perhaps even loosening of the joints. The wood itself has the flexibility needed. Overall the aim should be that the wood frame never needs restoring again under normal circumstances.'

Chip Kussmaul from Cincinnati Woodworks agrees with these views and adds:

The short answer is that I epoxy all joints. There is absolutely nothing stronger. A screw is only holding at the threads, whereas glue is holding along the entire surface. Also very importantly, epoxy completely seals water out of the joint, and that is perhaps as important as the strength of the joint. However, I only screw the panels in.

Back in the old days the joints were both screwed and glued. In my opinion, the screws were a back-up, based on the recognition that the glue would

eventually fail, whereas today's glues are superior and the screws aren't really necessary.

We use the West system, because in addition to quality, the system is very user friendly: you can buy simple push pumps that meter out the appropriate amounts of epoxy and catalyst, and there are fillers that allow you to create whatever level of 'stiffness' you desire. You can get fast or slow catalyst; I strongly recommend slow catalyst.

Powdered tempera, which is not available from West systems, can be added to get a desired colour. Doing this allows you to use the epoxy as a filler for damaged areas in old wood. Two advantages over traditional fillers are, first, it is glue and can help hold damaged wood together, and second, it has a translucency that looks more natural next to the wood than opaque fillers do.

It would seem that the screw and glue process is virtually universal, and

internationally accepted as the way forward. Peter van Heuvel, who is (at the time of writing) tackling a new-build woodie on a 1930s MG chassis, seems to have the last word on the subject:

I have glued and screwed most of the joints and they are now stiff without squeaking. I used this process when I made the new ash frame for my MG VA Tickford twelve years ago, and it is still stiff and squeak free after twenty thousand miles.

I use slotted stainless screws and one-component glue from Henkel Dores HD 024 – it's water-resistant, dries fast, and you get no dirty fingers when using it. All the plywood (end) sides and end parts of the ash I treat with a special clear paint to protect as much as possible against water ingress – though of course not the parts that you glue together. All the wood is also treated with a liquid against worm before the clear lacquer.

CHAPTER 11

How to Build Coachbuilt Cars

The term 'coachbuilt' has clear and definable routes going back to the age of the rudimentary horse-drawn coaches that were used to transport travellers to the four corners of the earth. Whilst early automobiles often took their styling cues, if we can call them that, from these early forms of transportation, coachbuilding in a true automotive sense really began to develop as an art form in the years that followed the Great War of 1914–18.

With literally thousands of small coachbuilders dotted around Britain, the country quickly led the style revolution that saw motor vehicles change from boxes on wheels to true style icons. Many so-called coachbuilders constructed trucks, buses and vans as well as cars, and while some of the construction and repair techniques being

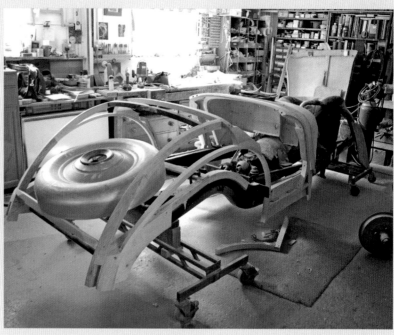

An Allard takes shape at Clanfield Coachbuilding.

This unique 1948 Bristol 400 was bodied from new with wooden sides resembling the style of a shooting brake, which allowed it to sidestep Draconian purchase tax laws that were in force in the UK at the time of its launch.

used to restore these vehicles in the twenty-first century might be similar, this section will focus exclusively on car bodywork.

One of the few positive legacies of the Great War was that a large number of people had, through necessity, become familiar with the operation of motor vehicles, and now actively created a demand for them following the cessation of hostilities. While the smaller, and cheaper, cars were often supplied with 'in-house' bodywork, manufacturers of quality chassis only ever supplied a rolling chassis, allowing the customer to have the vehicle bodied by a coachbuilder of their own choice or at one of the 'preferred' coachbuilders suggested by the chassis manufacturer.

Such was the competition between coachbuilders that style often took preference over functionality. Customers were often faced with such a vast array of body styles and number of doors, windows, seats and body coverings that many vehicles were unique – although it is fair to say that designs from the 1920s were still fairly conservative by comparison with those of the 1930s.

By the 1930s tall vertical lines had given way to low horizontal lines, and coachbuilders looked at the streamlined forms taking shape in the aircraft industry and tried to mirror their designs with a new breed of streamlined cars. However, despite their mixed fortunes, the coachbuilding industry struggled on with a mixed bag of clientèle.

On the other hand, volume automakers were increasingly moving the production of vehicle bodies in-house. The introduction of quick-drying cellulose paints in the mid-1920s allowed manufacturers to overcome the bottleneck previously caused by the use of slow-drying coach paints. However, it was the advent of large sheet-metal presses that sounded the death knell for 'batch-building' coachbuilders. These new presses meant that the automakers could, for the first time, press out wings/fenders, bonnets/hoods and even doors swiftly, accurately and cost effectively, and this soon led volume automakers to build all-steel car bodies in-house.

While the advent of World War II

didn't do the coachbuilding industry any favours, the industry didn't die as a result: it just went slowly into decline. Perhaps the most noticeable development, especially with regard to the content of this book, was the decline in the use of wood for car bodywork. Wood was one of the most plentiful raw products in Europe at the end of the war, and although coachbuilders turned their expertise to converting the widest range of war surplus vehicles into 'passenger carriers', the austerity years that followed provided limited opportunities for the industry to prosper.

The introduction of the factory-built, all-steel body had started pushing car coachbuilding firms towards oblivion, and the final nail in their coffin was surely the almost universal introduc-

tion of the chassisless unit body across the British and European car industry in the early 1950s. One of the most notable exceptions to this rule was the specialist sports car manufacturer Morgan, which carried on building wood-framed bodywork well into the twenty-first century.

A wooden coachbuilt body sits on a metal chassis as a separate structure, and does not have the structural integrity to allow fitting to any form of unit body vehicle. As regards its restoration there are both pluses and minuses. If we compare a typical coachbuilt saloon (or sedan in the USA) with, say, a wooden-bodied station wagon, virtually all the wood is hidden underneath some form of skin or panelling and it is therefore much easier to splice in repair sections.

The AC 2-litre saloon was one of the last mainstream coachbuilt cars constructed in the UK. Production ran from 1947 to 1958.

Once a wooden-framed car is deemed to need structural work, the only logical step is to remove its outer skin so the inner framework, or wooden skeleton, can be examined in detail.

The use of laminated structures is also common on coachbuilt cars, especially for curved components, and these may also be easier for the home restorer to construct. The station wagon, on the other hand, has all its bodywork on show and so it is harder to blend in repairs.

On the down side, the fact that the coachbuilt car usually has its wooden frame skinned in metal (usually aluminium) can fool the unwary into believing the body is in better shape than it really is. On a steel-framed bodywork we know to look for rust at panel edges and the supporting substructure, but a coachbuilt car can decay from the inside out, and rotten wood and joints may not be visible under a metal skin.

Joints can weaken and the body can lose its structural integrity yet appear superficially sound. In researching this chapter Peter Bayliss at Clanfield Coachbuilding showed me how the wooden A-pillar had rotted from the inside, which meant that the front doors sagged when open. The hinges had little to screw on to, so the front bulkhead had to be stripped of its panelling before remedial work could be tackled.

Once a wooden-framed car is considered to need structural work, the only logical step is to remove its outer skin so the inner framework, or wooden skeleton, can be examined in detail. If you happen to own one of the more popular makes of coachbuilt car, and particularly the open roadster variety such as MG, Morgan, Riley or Triumph, you are most likely to find complete repair sections available from the appropriate one-make owners club.

However, don't expect 'off the shelf' repair sections to fit without some fettling, as coachbuilt cars were all hand built, which means that there will be some slight differences in original fit and measurements. Once the exterior skin is peeled off the wooden frame you'll generally find a crude but effective structure, and then you'll be able to determine the amount of remedial work needed and whether you'll have to remove the body from the chassis.

TOP: *Removal of the outer panelling can be a complicated business. This two-door AC saloon has the roof, rear section, rear quarter panels and even the sills (rocker panels) all welded together and needs very careful storage so as not to crack any of the joints or stress the aluminium panels.*

LEFT: *In some cases it may be necessary to cut the rear section of panelling in half to remove it from the wooden frame.*

BELOW LEFT: *Once the panelling is removed it is essential to ensure that the old frame is level and square before taking any measurements or creating any templates.*

BELOW RIGHT: *Classic Restorations are seen here building the new Lagonda body alongside the old rotten shell. It has been retained for reference.*

If you do decide to lift the body off the chassis, it is essential to brace the structure, particularly the door gaps, to stop the body bowing out in the middle. You could attach wood or metal cross-bracing from the hinge mounting points, or you leave the doors in place to help avoid any distortion. Whether you decide to remove the body from the chassis, or undertake repair work in situ, it is essential to ensure that the body is square and level before starting any repair work or you may find that the panels no longer fit properly when you try to refit them.

Whatever timber you use to repair or rebuild the wooden frame will be expensive, but you'll be able to reduce the overall cost by splicing in repair sections wherever possible instead of fabricating entirely new structures. You'll also be able to save time and the arduous job of sawing and planing if you get your chosen timber supplier to run the lengths of wood through their planer/thicknesser so that you only have to shape it and cut it to length.

The AC 2-litre saloon is full of complex curves, but these are easy to replicate as each is made from more than one section.

Ian Strange has chosen to paint the wooden frame of his AC 2-litre saloon with an air-breathable polyurethane paint, which cleverly highlights the complicated sub-structure used to mount the wooden bodywork to the chassis frame.

This set of original metal 'sweeps' is used to measure and replicate set lines of curvature on bodywork. Longer wooden versions are seen underneath.

Long wooden sweeps can be used to check the longitudinal curvature of a vehicle body.

RIGHT: The sweep can be used to check that the curvature is correct lower down the body.

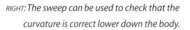

Here a metal sweep is used in conjunction with a longer wooden sweep to check both horizontal and vertical curvature lines.

The front bulkhead/firewall area of wooden-framed cars is a common problem area, and this example shows typical damage and cracking. The only sensible option is to replace this with new wood.

Many wooden doors had steel edging nailed on to give them a sharper edge for folding the aluminium panelling around.

Before building a new body it is essential to establish the centre line of the chassis, and mark out datum points from that to ensure that all future bodywork sits square and level. These triangular frames ensure the centre line can be carried across the top of the bodywork.

The centre line at the rear of the car was marked on a chassis cross-member and then transferred to the wooden body buck using a plumb line.

By using an inner body buck the templates used to locate outer framework can be transferred, or replicated, on both sides of the body to ensure 100 per cent accurate alignment.

When constructing new convertible bodywork it may be necessary or desirable to construct an inner body buck out of plywood to help support the outer frame while it is under construction, and also to ensure that all body shapes, angles and forms are correctly transferred from the old body.

Steaming was a time-consuming and expensive process to undertake so most coachbuilders perfected the art of splicing wood together to form complex curves.

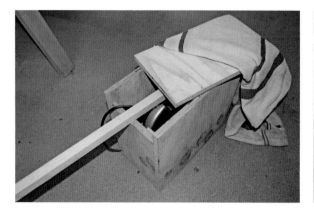

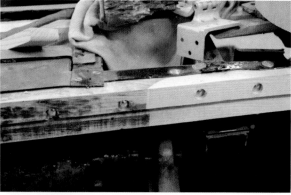

TOP LEFT: *This simple but effective steamer is basically a plywood box into which is placed an electric kettle and the top covered over with a sheet of plywood and a towel. There's a slit at each through which a length of ash can be passed. This crude steamer apparently allows ash to bend as much as a half inch.*

TOP RIGHT: *The restorer, and/or newbuilder, should have no qualms about splicing new wood into old to affect a repair.*

LEFT: *The front hinge area is a common rot area on wooden-bodied vehicles. The front door was relatively sound on this car, but the hinge area had decayed so a new section was spliced in allowing the doors to open without dropping.*

On the right front side the hinge area on the A-post had decayed so new wood has been spliced in.

The bottom hinge section of the front door had also decayed, so a new section was shaped and spliced in.

Depending on the level of decay or damage to the frame, it may be possible to facilitate a simple repair by relocating a hinge an inch or so.

RIGHT: The internal structure of this door was retained to keep the original shape and dimensions, but a new outside edge was spliced in to ensure the door aligned perfectly with the B post.

A useful tip is to keep a selection of offcuts of various thicknesses and sizes of wood and plywood, as these will help simplify the marking up of cut lines.

Here we can see the complete door with sections of new wood carefully spliced in.

And don't forget those drain holes in the bottom of the doors!

Whilst endeavouring to mimic the style and construction methods true to the original, sometimes 'modern' thinking is the way to go. The original coachbuilder of this saloon used spliced sections to create the curvature around the rear mudguards. However, it is much easier to form the replacement by laminating strips together – especially as it will be hidden from view.

As mentioned previously, laminated sections can be made up to form wheel arches and structural sections such as sills, and almost any section that is curved. By bonding several thin pieces together you'll end up with a structure that is stronger than those made from a single piece of wood. When forming laminated sections you need at least ten cramps to hold the pieces firmly together and you should use sections that are slightly wider than required so that you can lightly plane the bonded structure smooth and to the required width.

Whether your laminations are large or small, you'll need to make a former around which the glue-coated strips will be pulled and cramped in place. Remember to use polythene sheeting between the former and the laminations, or it may all be bonded together permanently.

Most coachbuilt cars had wooden floors. Some used planks whilst others had flat boards, but whatever you choose, remember to use either marine or exterior grade wood as it will take a lot of punishment from being close to the road and exposed to the elements. You might also want to consider building in access panels during the rebuild in case you need to create easier access to gearbox filler caps or pedal linkages.

Plywood is usually found in coachbuilt vehicles, most commonly for panels (interior as well as exterior) and quite often for floors. If you need to join boards end-grain to end-grain you will get a much stronger bond if the joint runs diagonally across the board.

The large rear mudguards on this Allard roadster require a lengthy wooden wheel arch, which is much easier to re-create using laminated strips.

The original wheel arch on this Bentley was steamed into shape, but it's easier to make the replacement from laminations glued together, which will actually be stronger than the original.

This shot shows how to make the template of the curvature of the wheel arch out of MDF.

We've previously touched on the use of wood preservatives and wood treatments (*see* Chapter 9), and as the wood frame will (in most cases) be panelled over, you could even use some of the coloured wood treatments, which will give you a visible check on achieving total coverage. Do not, however, be tempted to coat the wooden structure with regular household paint, as this will stop it breathing and terminally shorten its useful lifespan.

We've also touched on the use of screws and glues in the previous chapter, but it's worth noting a great tip mentioned by Brian Cox, when writing about replacing wood frames in *Practical Classics* magazine, back in 2000. Brian advises that only zinc-plated or stainless steel screws should be used, as the heads of brass screws tend to shear off under pressure. He also recommends coating screws with either soap, petroleum jelly or anti-rust wax before inserting them, as this will make them screw in much more easily. However, don't be tempted to use engine oil as a coating as it will seep into the timber and affect adhesion.

Some restorers even recommend using epoxy adhesive on the screws for a really good strong joint – although getting them apart at some future date might just be an issue.

The MDF templates can then be glued together to the required thickness equivalent to the width of wheel arch you need to replicate.

The MDF template/former being used in situ to create the laminated wheel-arch sections.

TOP LEFT: *Many coachbuilt cars, such as this AC, had wooden floorboards so replacements need to be both strong and protected against dampness.*

TOP RIGHT: *It goes without saying that all screw heads should be countersunk.*

LEFT: *The bodywork on this Bentley coupé de ville shows just how many angles and joints go to make up a high quality coachbuilt body.*

Even screw heads on hardware and fittings should be countersunk to avoid damage to metal or fabric covering.

The bodywork on this MG L-type coupé is in the mock-up stage and most major sections are just clamped together to ensure everything lines up before final assembly takes place.

The B-pillar and internal cross-bracing is just a temporary structure to support the roof sections until the rear wheel arch is in place and the real B-pillar can be installed.

Gary Tuffnell at Classic Restorations uses thin pieces of MDF to hold the joints of the temporary internal cross-bracing during the mock-up stage.

Use a spirit level and a plumb line to ensure that the structure is both square and level.

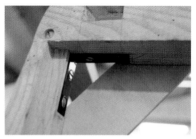

On curved sections where it may prove difficult to cut a correctly aligned tenon it may be possible to insert a separate tenon or 'biscuit' into a groove cut into the end of the frame section.

Small metal brackets can be recessed into joints for extra strength.

BOLTING IT TOGETHER

One of the most often overlooked aspects of a coachbuilt body is the bolts holding things together. It goes without saying that all screw heads should be countersunk, but there will be sections that are either bolted together or bolted to the metal frame. AC 2-litre restoration expert Ian Strange has some strong views on the subject, and advises that you should not mix nuts and bolts that have different threadforms, even if they appear to fit the hole.

It's hard to image that this rotten piece of timber was once a major structural component.

The original rear aluminium panelling is seen here clipped in place to help determine correct body lines. The two-door coupé bodywork has doors that continue into the rear wheel arch, and once this is in position the new rear B-pillar can be put into place.

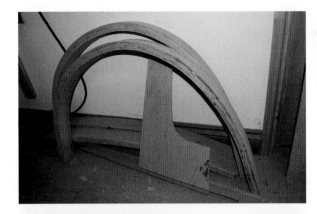

The rear wheel arches for the MG coupé were laminated from thin strips of ash.

The rear wing can be used to check the shape and the fit of the new wheel arches.

Every restorer seems to have a different opinion of which preservative to use on the wooden frame. Classic Restoration's Garry Tuffnell prefers blackboard paint.

With so many threadforms (both fine and coarse) used on British, European and American vehicles over the years, plus the recent move to metric bolts, sourcing the right size and correct strength nuts and bolts is something of a minefield. A good hardware store or specialist should be able to advise you on the codes used on the heads of bolts, because with so much cheap hardware coming out of south-east Asia you really need to use the highest quality and strength available, as your life could literally depend on it.

When building the framework for a coachbuilt vehicle it is essential that you give thought as to how the vehicle will be panelled so as to avoid any bolts, screws or frame edges actually touching and/or rubbing against the panels. This could cause creases or dents that will ultimately show up on painted surfaces and detract from the finished restoration.

The only exception to this rule is where the ends of the panel are fixed to the frame. Ian Strange advises that it is common practice for aluminium panels to be secured with hundreds of panel pins, and reminds us that these pins often need to be inserted near the edges of wood frame components and so should be inserted at an angle to reduce the likelihood of the wood frame splitting. Drilling pilot holes may help, especially if the wood is beech, which is prone to splitting. He concludes: 'Galvanized pins might be a good idea, and possibly dipping them in an anti-corrosion wax. However, stainless steel pins might cause the alloy panelling to corrode by electrolytic action and so are not advisable.'

CHAPTER 12

How to Build Shooting Brakes

The term 'shooting brake' is still banded around today by some modern-day automakers, who seem to think the term can breathe new life into a tired old estate car range. In fact most car makers and buyers alike seem to have forgotten that the term was born in the 1920s and was used to describe the original sport utility vehicle (shooting refers to hunting) in an era when the line between cars, vans and light commercials was very distinct.

My interest in the subject began in 1998 when I discovered a wooden-bodied 1950 Austin A70 Countryman estate car on a web site in Canada and thought it would make an interesting restoration project. After shipping the car back to the UK I delved into the background of such vehicles and found that the survival rate of wooden-bodied shooting brakes, estate cars and station wagons, generically known as woodies, was pitifully low in the UK. Exposed wooden framework (usually ash) and utility construction, coupled

Woodies were built in all shapes and sizes and on just about every conceivable chassis, such as this diminutive 1932 twin-cylinder Jowett.

The term 'estate car' is derived from the fact that woodies were used as the fetch-and-carry vehicle for large country estates.

with a necessity for revarnishing every couple of years to keep the damp out, meant that few examples completed their first decade without terminal decay setting in.

Historically, the two biggest markets for woodies were the USA and the UK. While US woodies can trace their origins back to the open-sided 'depot hacks' (the name derived from the connection with railroad depots), which were the forerunners of the modern-day taxicab, British 'shooting brakes', on the other hand, were originally built for conveying wealthy land owners and their guests on shooting parties.

BIRTH OF THE UTILITY VEHICLE

While Rolls-Royce was the chassis of choice for builders of those early shooting brakes, during the 1930s cheap Canadian-built Ford V8 utilities were imported to the UK and set the scene for the utility or dual-purpose vehicle that was part car, part van and even part bus.

By the late 1930s most manufacturers were supplying chassis to specialist coachbuilders, and it was not unusual for humble Fords, Austins and Hillmans to end up as utility estate cars. While the term 'shooting brake' had become

generic by this time, many woodies were built strictly as utility vehicles. Names such as Brakenvan, Utilicon and Utilibrake had a much more workaday purpose, and the ability to carry both passengers and goods gave them a wider public appeal.

It must also be remembered that shooting brakes and utility brakes were legally classified as commercial vehicles in the UK, and therefore restricted to a maximum speed of 30mph on any road! A contemporary road test in *Autocar* magazine of the then new 1937 Ford V8 woodie speaks volumes of passenger comfort, luggage-carrying capacity and the vehicle's ability to gobble up mile after mile with ease, with an effortless 60mph cruising speed. The same report also mentions the tester's continuing worry about being stopped by every village policeman he passed for exceeding the 30mph speed limit for light commercials.

While woodies followed a fairly slow and natural course of evolution during the 1930s, the outbreak of World War II in Europe during 1939 saw the introduction of tough new legal measures in the UK, which were to change the course of woodie history. The first of these measures was the introduction of petrol rationing, so that more fuel could be diverted to the war effort.

The initial allowance for private motoring equated – depending on the model of car – to enough fuel to cover between 100 and 200 miles a month. Commercial vehicles, on the other hand, were given a larger allowance, which suddenly made ownership of a shooting brake (legally classified as a commercial vehicle) a rather more attractive proposition.

TAX EXEMPTION FOR WOODIES

By July 1940 the British government had taken over stocks of all new cars and summarily banned their purchase by private individuals, except under special circumstances. By October that year the production of private cars was halted altogether, so that automakers could give their undivided attention to the production of heavy equipment for the war effort. At the same time the British government introduced a new form of retail taxation, known as purchase tax. This was levied at 33 per cent on the price of all new cars (providing, of course, you could lay your hands on one), but not on commercial vehicles – another major plus point for owning a woodie.

In the years that followed a number of perfectly sound saloon cars – providing they had not already been

Even Commer, which was the truck and van division of the Rootes Group, aimed its Commer Tender at the hunting and estate transport fraternity.

RIGHT: This 1936 Ford UK advert describes the Ford utility car as the 'Sportsman's Pullman', and the uniformed driver highlights the upmarket clientele it was aimed at.

Whilst early shooting brakes were built largely on upmarket chassis such as Rolls-Royce, very few Bentleys acquired wooden bodies.

Some smaller British manufacturers such as Lea-Francis found that chassis production often outstripped the supply of metal for bodies, so building wooden-bodied utility vehicles was the perfect answer.

requisitioned for War Department service – were driven, or most likely pushed, into the workshops of local coachbuilders across the UK. They would then have the rear half of the body cut off and replaced with more appropriate commercial bodywork. Many were converted into wooden-bodied utilities, since with supplies of metal being diverted to the war effort, the conversion of ash-framed bodywork was a simple 'screw and glue' job.

Some of these conversions were crude, while others were on a par with the work of the best coachbuilders. Many of the larger engined, gas-guzzling 6- and 8-cylinder North American cars, such as Buick, Dodge, Hudson, Plymouth, Packard and Studebaker – that were so popular on pre-war British roads – were summarily converted in this way. Many large cars were also requisitioned by the War Department and were turned into ambulances, mobile canteens, vans and even light trucks. Once hostilities ceased and these service vehicles were no longer needed to perform the same role, then it was relatively easy for private individuals to have such vehicles rebuilt as wooden-bodied shooting brakes.

SHORTAGE OF CONVENTIONAL BODIES

The first post-war government budget was issued in 1945, and this saw the retention of purchase tax (PT) on private cars at 33 per cent, while commercials and shooting brake derivatives remained exempt.

A number of factors combined to make woodies an extremely popular mode of transport during this time. Firstly, Britain had a rich heritage of small commercial coachbuilding firms whose experience in building van, truck and bus bodies made them perfectly placed to capitalize on the demand for new vehicles. While there were severe restrictions on the availability of new cars, there were no such restrictions on new commercial chassis and chassis cabs, and this provided the basis for large numbers of woodies.

In fact many small and specialized manufacturers, such as Alvis and Lea-Francis, found that chassis production often outstripped the supply of bodies. The solution was to supply chassis direct to local coachbuilders to have wooden-framed utility bodies built.

Many leading car dealers also had contracts with local coachbuilders, whose work usually went unacknowledged. Automakers also took to branding their factory-approved estate cars as 'utility' models in their advertising and literature, as if to reaffirm their tax-free status.

However, the quality of workmanship, and particularly the materials used to construct some of the woodies produced to exploit this tax loophole, was often suspect. Some utility vehicles were built as cheaply as possible, often with opening rear side doors omitted or sealed shut, and the fitting of rear doors instead of split tailgates. Lea-Francis took the 'utility' theme a stage further and built woodie vans, many of which omitted rear seats and side windows completely. These vans could be, and frequently were, later upgraded to estate car specification.

FACTORY-APPROVED WOODIES

Austin was one of the first British manufacturers to launch its own factory-approved woodie, after tying up a deal for the construction of 500 Austin 16 shooting brakes with

Austin was one of the first British manufacturers to launch its own factory-approved woodie, after tying up a deal for the construction of 500 Austin 16 shooting brakes with Papworth Industries in Cambridgeshire.

More than 5,000 Morris MO Oxford Travellers were built between 1952 and 1954, but only an estimated twenty-five to thirty survive worldwide. This example was restored by Frank Healey in Australia.

The Morris Minor Traveller was launched in 1953 as the Oxford Traveller's little brother. It was a huge success, and production lasted until 1971.

A number of US woodie builders can provide 'flat pack' bodies shipped to your door, like these 1949–51 Ford items from Richard McCloskey at Rickmack.com.

Papworth Industries in Cambridgeshire in 1948. While Alvis didn't offer its own 'approved' woodie, Lea-Francis did. After having a number of 14hp chassis bodied by a variety of bodybuilders, the Coventry-based car maker contracted AP Aircraft of Coventry to build its regular saloon bodies, as well as a large number of 'utility' shooting brakes. Records show that more than 1,000 such vehicles were constructed between 1945 and 1954.

The car-derived Austin A70 Hampshire pick-up chassis cab proved particularly popular during this time, and a number of bodybuilders emulated the A70 Countryman that Papworth Industries built after Austin had ceased production of the 16. It was a time when everything from Bristols and Bradfords through to Willys and Wolseleys ended up as woodie estates. I've not yet come across a Foden or a Scammell bodied as a woodie, but that's only surely a matter of time.

One of the first post-war legislative changes to affect the future of the woodie came in 1947 when purchase tax was introduced for the first time

on all estate cars. Some manufacturers responded by finding loopholes in the law, which allowed them to modify bodywork so that the vehicle conformed much closer to a description laid down for commercial vehicles and thus continue their tax-free status. Such modifications included reducing the number of side-opening doors from four to three – usually achieved by fixing the offside rear side door in the shut position – replacing the rear tailgates with doors and removing the rear seats.

THE BEGINNING OF THE END

After decades of building vehicles with separate chassis and bodies, the British motor industry increasingly moved over to the mass production of unitary construction cars in the early 1950s – and this, more than anything else, finally killed off the coachbuilt woodie.

Sales of woodies had never been high when compared to the volumes achieved by saloon cars, and when purchase tax was imposed on com-

mercial vehicles for the first time in April 1950 some manufacturers saw sales fall even further. Both Alvis and Lea-Francis were hard hit, yet Austin soldiered on until 1954 when the last separate chassis A70 Countryman rolled off the Papworth production line in Cambridgeshire.

Although the era of the British coachbuilt woodie ended at this time, the previous year Morris Motors had introduced its mass-produced Minor Traveller, which was to make woodies available to the masses – but that's another story.

Just as with the coachbuilt car, as discussed previously, the wooden-bodied estate car, station wagon or shooting brake, generically known as woodies today, is also something of a Catch 22. Visually pleasing when in good order, the very fact that the entire body frame is exposed and open to the elements meant that they were high maintenance vehicles when new, and the fact that owners were not prepared to apply a fresh coat of varnish every few years is one of the main reasons that so few survive today.

The first place to start with a major restoration project is to assess what you have, and determine whether you are going to repair or replace.

As discussed in previous chapters, woodies tend to decompose due to wood rot and bug infestations, and major failings tend to occur in joints and from the bottom up. So it is not uncommon for a car with rotten body-work to have a roof structure in perfectly sound condition.

With literally hundreds of body styles constructed over the years by as many different coachbuilders, bodybuilders, truck and bus builders and even individuals, the first place to start with a major restoration is to assess what you have and determine whether you are going to repair or replace. American-built woodies are today supported by a number of specialists (many of whom have contributed to this book) who can supply you with everything from an individual body part to a complete, fully fitted body or turnkey car. Many will even ship you a 'flat pack' body for self-assembly.

So, if you have a vehicle for which a new body is available and you've decided to go down that route then you'll want to remove the old body from the chassis in its entirety. However, if you are just making repairs, replacing some sections or have a vehicle where no off-the-shelf body parts are available, then the last thing you'll want to do is to rush into removing the whole body structure.

Most factory (aka mass-produced) woodie bodies used some form of metal floor pan to which the wood structure was attached. Coachbuilt vehicles, on the other hand, tend to have wooden floors as they usually had to start with a bare chassis. This latter process can result in some complicated sub-structure being built in order to provide a secure basis for the upper structure to have something to attach to.

Some woodies did not stand up to the ravages of time very well, but they can always be rebuilt as good if not better than new, providing you have the time and patience!

Most mass-produced/factory-built woodies were usually constructed on the steel floorpan of the saloon or convertible.

The starting point for restoring the bodywork on any coachbuilt vehicle has to be to ensure that the chassis frame is both square and level. The fact that coachbuilt vehicle bodies were hand built usually means that no two vehicles have exactly the same dimensions, so starting with a straight and level base will help to reduce any alignment and dimensional problems later in the build.

Because the scale of the bodywork on most woodies is quite large you need to give plenty of thought to supporting the structure (or what's left of it) before starting off the restoration process. I have previously constructed an X brace out of square metal tubing, which was tack welded together in the centre and screwed to the hinge points either side on both the B and C pillars.

Most coachbuilders started with a chassis cowl/scuttle and had to construct their own wooden sub-structure on which to mount the bodywork.

In most cases you'll almost certainly want to remove the roof structure before tackling any repairs or replacement, as it usually locks most of the uprights into place.

The side roof rails on this Morris Oxford Traveller are so badly decomposed that they have virtually broken in two.

This ensured the sides stayed firmly and squarely in place when I removed the roof.

Most woodies have a substantial roof structure and, depending on the condition of the supporting framework, you might want to remove it to give better access to the frame. Every coachbuilder used different fixing techniques, but I know from my experience of working on both Austin and early Ford woodies that the roof generally holds the sides in place, and it would be difficult to remove uprights or whole rear side sections without first removing the roof, or at least jacking it up.

You'll need at least two, if not three people to help you lift the roof off the car without damaging anything, and you'll probably want to construct some sort of trestle to lay it on, once it is removed. I have seen images where a wooden roof has been lifted off using some sort of pulley system to raise it up into the garage roof, but I must admit to having no working knowledge of how efficient such a system might be. Further, if the roof, pulleys and rope used are strong enough, this could be a great way to store the woodie's roof

without it taking up floor space in the garage.

We've already covered the teardown, repairing, preserving process in previous chapters, so let's jump straight to the construction and assembly process. This will also assume, unless otherwise stated, that we are now focusing on completely new wood sections.

As stated earlier, part of the magic of a woodie is in the beauty of its wood, and studying grain patterns will help you enhance that natural beauty. Ash, for instance, can present a fine straight grain on one surface whilst having a beautiful wavy pattern on the adjacent surface, depending on how the wood was sawn. Sadly, however, most coachbuilders of yesteryear were more concerned with turning out a finished product than selecting wood for pleasing grain patterns, which accounts for the fact that most woodies will have a mix of grain patterns throughout.

Maple is a popular choice for North American woodies, and generally it has a less distinctive but finer grain pattern than ash, although the speckled effect of bird's eye maple is certainly both distinctive and attractive. When

woodies were being built in America, sections of bird's eye maple would be mixed in with regular long-grain maple, and my own Ford woodie has a couple of bird's eye pieces mixed in amongst its construction. I believe that Ford stockpiled bird's eye maple for a while, which allowed it to build a small number of woodies completely out of this type, but I have yet to see one, so can't say how attractive the overall result might be.

The logical place to start the restoration is with the bare frame stripped of doors, tailgates and roof – these can be worked on separately. If you just have one section to replace then you can use that piece to act as a pattern when shaping a new piece on the bandsaw. However, if a substantial part of the frame has rotted away or is missing, then you should cut templates around fenders or door frames out of card, or even plywood, to get the size, shape and curvature of the missing section before removing the part.

Should the part you need to replace be in such a poor state of decomposition that there's a real risk of it crumbling away to a pile of splinters should

The logical place to start any restoration is with all panels, doors, glass and tailgates removed, as there's no point doing any remedial work elsewhere until the main frame is 100 per cent.

Most US-built woodies used finger joints in their construction, which many home restorers find difficult to replicate. Steve, at Cincinnati Woodworks, is seen here cutting finger joints on a milling machine: this cuts three fingers at a time and with 1/1000in accuracy, so it's easy to reposition accurately for additional fingers.

Here, Cincinnati's milling machine is working with a mortiser to cut the mortise in the top of the rear corner post of a 1946–48 Ford woodie.

The main structure of a woodie takes its shape, and gets its strength, from the rear section of the bodywork, so this is a logical place to start the rebuild. Here we see the remnants of the rear section and rear door (as opposed to a tailgate) serving as a pattern to shape new parts.

Most popular makes of American woodies are supported by specialists who can supply a complete 'flat pack' body for you to assemble in your own garage. However, owners of European and less popular makes will have to make their own replacement parts.

With the new wood securely in place the body has both tensile strength and form on which other parts can be based.

This shot shows the importance of the rear quarter panels in providing the body with overall structural integrity.

Once the rear quarters degrade, the rest of the body starts to go out of shape. This Austin 16 Countryman has had the back end rebuilt using everything including parts of a garden shed, judging by this shot.

The body of this 1937 Austin 18 was in very poor structural condition, but once the chassis had been levelled and the front half of the body supported, the important rear quarter sections could be rebuilt to provide integrity for the rest of the body.

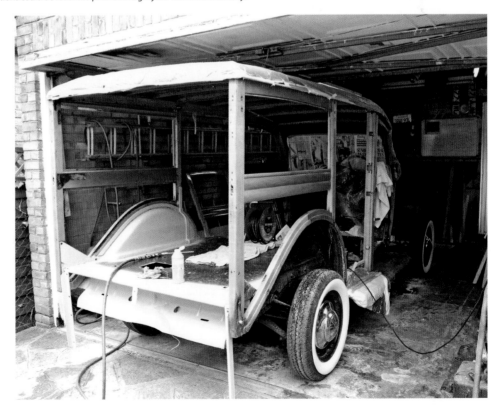

Rear wings are usually held in place by a series of studs. This is a good time to check their alignment and weld in new ones to replace any that are damaged or broken. It's also a good time to check on the workings of lower tailgate hinge mechanisms, as these could be difficult to access once assembly of the rear commences.

The images of this unique coachbuilt three-door Morris Minor Traveller show how the body frame is tied together to form the basic structure.

Station wagons and estate cars were constructed with a wide variety of rear ends. Single or twin doors and opening tailgates provided both form and access.

Two different versions of rear end bodywork on Lea-Francis woodies, both with twin rear doors.

Ford wagons have a massive, almost truck-like lower tailgate, but three rows of seats severely restrict luggage capacity (unless you were prepared to tie it to the tailgate).

The rear load space can be enhanced with the fitting of aluminium rubbing strips on the tailgate, floor and rear seat back.

The tailgate frames on the 1950 Austin are quite flimsy and rely on structural integrity from exterior and interior plywood panels. Metal brackets were added to the corners for extra rigidity.

The upper tailgate on most woodies can become quite heavy – sometimes weighing 30–40lb – once fitted with new safety glass and hardware. Weak and flimsy joints can allow the tailgate to break apart, so this writer prefers to install all new wood to be safe. This image also shows a new top rail on to which the tailgate hinge will be affixed.

Trial fit. After installing a new or repaired tailgate it's worth bolting it on for a trial fit before varnishing, panelling and glazing.

The finished job, fully glazed and complete with hardware, neatly complements the rear of the car.

Repairing or constructing doors can present woodie restorers with some of their biggest challenges. Numerous parts make up a typical door, and it has to open and close and fit perfectly into the space it occupies. It also has to contain some sort of window mechanism, and many of the bodywork design cues are taken from the door.

The unique design of this front door sets the tone for the whole car.

It's very easy to construct a door that goes out of alignment. Many restorers not only undertake numerous trial fittings, but also prefer to do the final gluing and assembly of the doors within the door frame itself to ensure that the door retains its shape and is a perfect fit for the frame once the glue is dry.

The outer edge of the door should be higher than the inner edge so as to seal closely to the door frame, thus providing protection against the elements. You may also want to attach some sort of weather protection strip either on the door edge or on the frame itself to minimize draughts.

Screws holding the roof slats should be countersunk so there are no raised heads to rub against the roof lining and covering. Note the container of linseed oil (no, it's not a glass of beer!) being used by Phil Robertson here on the roof of the Railton newbuild woodie. He tells us that linseed oil helps to ease the screwing-in process, and allows powered drills and screwdrivers to operate at a lower torque setting.

On the home straight … once all the woodwork is constructed (and refinished) you can think about bolting on the sheet metalwork.

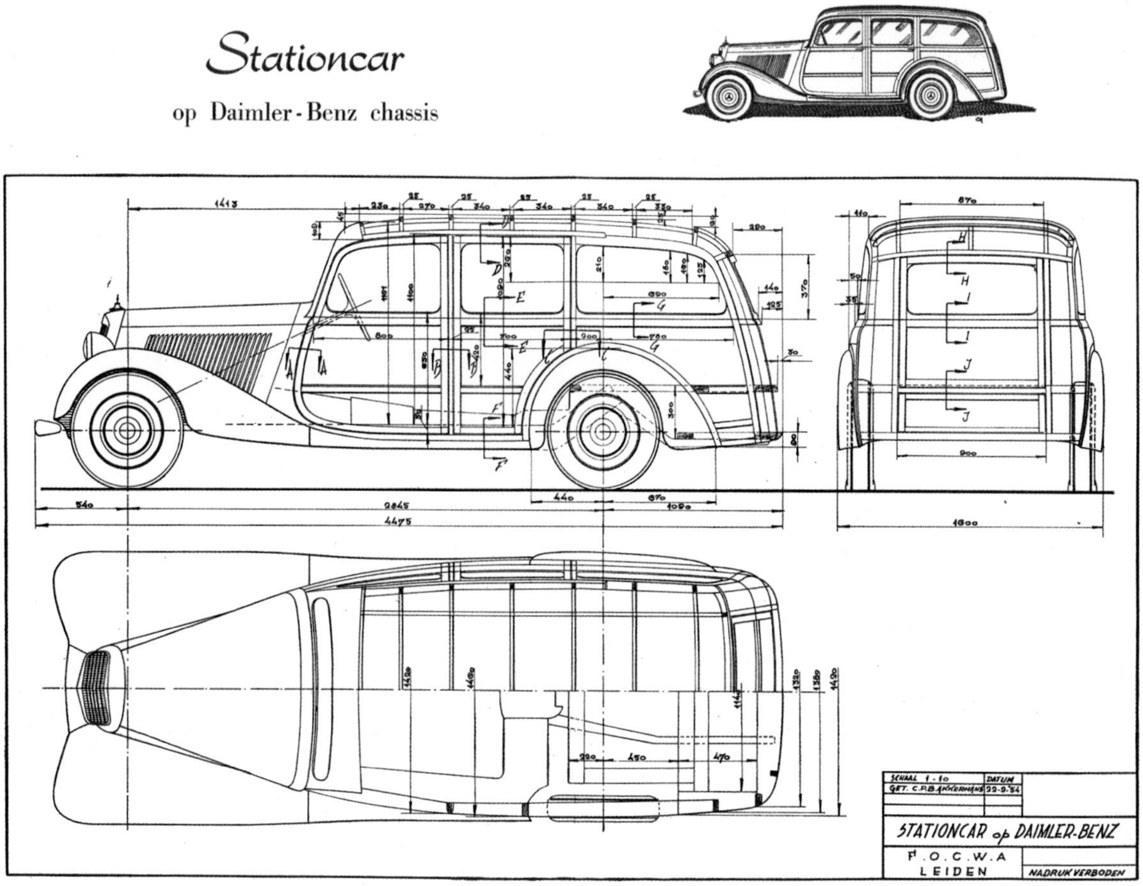
Stationcar
op Daimler-Benz chassis
SCHAAL 1:10
DATUM
GET. C.P.B. AKKERMANS 22-9-'54
STATIONCAR op DAIMLER-BENZ
F[a] .O.C.W.A
LEIDEN
NADRUK VERBODEN

These Stationcar plans for a Mercedes-Benz 170 were produced in Holland in 1954.

you try to remove it, then you could try brushing a layer of extra strong glue over the structure. When dry, this should enable you to remove the section keeping the general dimensions, curvatures and integrity together long enough for you to use it as a template from which to cut a new section.

This process will enable you to 'add' the missing section to the frame without the risk of getting the angles and dimensions wrong and so just creating more expensive scrap for the wood pile. I previously touched on the making and use of templates, and it's logical to make these before you start dismantling any rotten woodwork so that you can retain reference to the original dimensions and shape.

Lastly I am including two sets of plans in this chapter to help you visualize the construction process and hopefully get further inspired. Both date from the 1950s and give an insight into techniques and methods used back in those days.

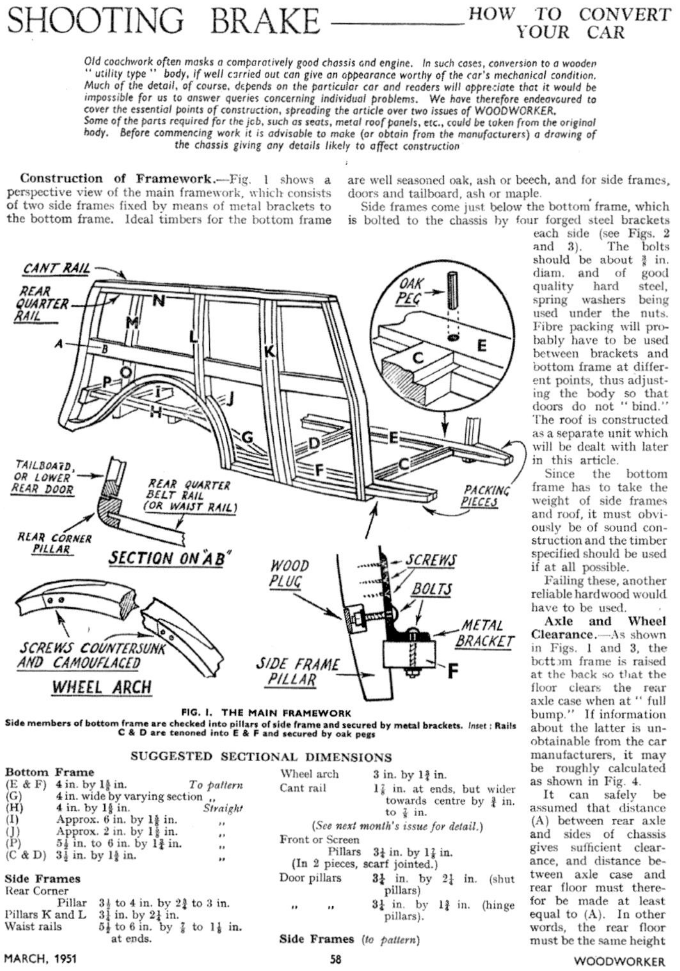

SHOOTING BRAKE —— HOW TO CONVERT YOUR CAR

Old coachwork often masks a comparatively good chassis and engine. In such cases, conversion to a wooden "utility type" body, if well carried out can give an appearance worthy of the car's mechanical condition. Much of the detail, of course, depends on the particular car and readers will appreciate that it would be impossible for us to answer queries concerning individual problems. We have therefore endeavoured to cover the essential points of construction, spreading the article over two issues of WOODWORKER. Some of the parts required for the job, such as seats, metal roof panels, etc., could be taken from the original body. Before commencing work it is advisable to make (or obtain from the manufacturers) a drawing of the chassis giving any details likely to affect construction

Construction of Framework.—Fig. 1 shows a perspective view of the main framework, which consists of two side frames fixed by means of metal brackets to the bottom frame. Ideal timbers for the bottom frame are well seasoned oak, ash or beech, and for side frames, doors and tailboard, ash or maple.

Side frames come just below the bottom frame, which is bolted to the chassis by four forged steel brackets each side (see Figs. 2 and 3). The bolts should be about $\frac{3}{8}$ in. diam. and of good quality hard steel, spring washers being used under the nuts. Fibre packing will probably have to be used between brackets and bottom frame at different points, thus adjusting the body so that doors do not "bind." The roof is constructed as a separate unit which will be dealt with later in this article.

Since the bottom frame has to take the weight of side frames and roof, it must obviously be of sound construction and the timber specified should be used if at all possible.

Failing these, another reliable hardwood would have to be used.

Axle and Wheel Clearance.—As shown in Figs. 1 and 3, the bottom frame is raised at the back so that the floor clears the rear axle case when at "full bump." If information about the latter is unobtainable from the car manufacturers, it may be roughly calculated as shown in Fig. 4.

It can safely be assumed that distance (A) between rear axle and sides of chassis gives sufficient clearance, and distance between axle case and rear floor must therefor be made at least equal to (A). In other words, the rear floor must be the same height

CANT RAIL
REAR QUARTER RAIL
A B M N L K O P I J H G D E F C
OAK PEG
E C
TAILBOARD, OR LOWER REAR DOOR
REAR QUARTER BELT RAIL (OR WAIST RAIL)
PACKING PIECES
REAR CORNER PILLAR
SECTION ON "AB"
WOOD PLUG
SCREWS
BOLTS
METAL BRACKET
F
SCREWS COUNTERSUNK AND CAMOUFLAGED
WHEEL ARCH
SIDE FRAME PILLAR

FIG. I. THE MAIN FRAMEWORK
Side members of bottom frame are checked into pillars of side frame and secured by metal brackets. *Inset* **: Rails C & D are tenoned into E & F and secured by oak pegs**

SUGGESTED SECTIONAL DIMENSIONS

Bottom Frame

(E & F)	4 in. by $1\frac{5}{8}$ in.	*To pattern*
(G)	4 in. wide by varying section	,,
(H)	4 in. by $1\frac{5}{8}$ in.	*Straight*
(I)	Approx. 6 in. by $1\frac{5}{8}$ in.	,,
(J)	Approx. 2 in. by $1\frac{5}{8}$ in.	,,
(P)	$5\frac{1}{2}$ in. to 6 in. by $1\frac{3}{4}$ in.	,,
(C & D)	$3\frac{1}{2}$ in. by $1\frac{5}{8}$ in.	,,

Side Frames

Rear Corner Pillar	$3\frac{1}{2}$ to 4 in. by $2\frac{3}{4}$ to 3 in.
Pillars K and L	$3\frac{1}{4}$ in. by $2\frac{1}{4}$ in.
Waist rails	$5\frac{1}{2}$ to 6 in. by $\frac{7}{8}$ to $1\frac{1}{8}$ in. at ends.
Wheel arch	3 in. by $1\frac{3}{4}$ in.
Cant rail	$1\frac{7}{8}$ in. at ends, but wider towards centre by $\frac{3}{8}$ in. to $\frac{7}{8}$ in.

(*See next month's issue for detail.*)

Front or Screen Pillars	$3\frac{1}{4}$ in. by $1\frac{7}{8}$ in. (In 2 pieces, scarf jointed.)
Door pillars	$3\frac{1}{4}$ in. by $2\frac{1}{4}$ in. (shut pillars)
,, ,,	$3\frac{1}{4}$ in. by $1\frac{3}{4}$ in. (hinge pillars).

Side Frames (*to pattern*)

MARCH, 1951 58 WOODWORKER

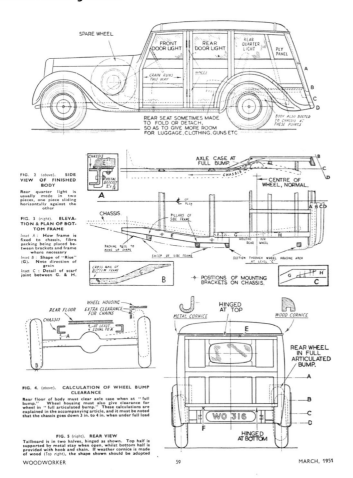

FIG. 2 (above). SIDE VIEW OF FINISHED BODY

Rear quarter light is usually made in two pieces, one piece sliding horizontally against the other

FIG. 3 (right). ELEVATION & PLAN OF BOTTOM FRAME

Inset A: How frame is fixed to chassis, fibre packing being placed between brackets and frame where necessary

Inset B: Shape of "Rise" (G). Note direction of grain

Inset C: Detail of scarf joint between G. & H.

FIG. 4. (above). CALCULATION OF WHEEL BUMP CLEARANCE

Rear floor of body must clear axle case when at "full bump." Wheel housing must also give clearance for wheel in "full articulated bump." These calculations are explained in the accompanying article, and it must be noted that the chassis goes down 3 in. to 4 in. when under full load

FIG. 5 (right). REAR VIEW

Tailboard is in two halves, hinged as shown. Top half is supported by metal stay when open, whilst bottom half is provided with hook and chain. If weather cornice is made of wood (Top right), the shape shown should be adopted

sides of rebates is essential to allow for movement of the panelling. It is usual for the outside grain of the panelling to run horizontally.

Wheel arch: This is made in three pieces scarf-jointed together, as in Fig. 1. It is tenoned and oak pegged to the rear corner pillar, and its other end is secured by a metal bracket to the side member of bottom frame. Pillar (L) is halved at its bottom end to the inside of the wheel arch, and is screwed.

Waterproof synthetic resin glue is recommended for all joints, but there are alternatives, depending on the particular finish given to the coachwork.

The second and concluding part of the shooting brake build feature and plans is from the April 1951 issue of *The Woodworker* magazine, and is reproduced by kind permission of the magazine.

Just as in the previous month, the magazine chose to run the final couple of paragraphs on a separate page, so we'll include them here:

The first plan shows how to construct a wooden 'station car' body on a Mercedes-Benz 170 chassis, while the second plan is part of an in-depth feature from the March 1951 edition of *The Woodworker* magazine, which has a detailed step-by-step feature on how to construct the generic shooting-brake body of what appears to be a Bentley or similar. The feature is reproduced in its entirety by kind permission of *The Woodworker* magazine, so drift back to a time before electric tools…

This editorial is a real time warp and highlights the fact that individuals were being encouraged to recycle older, and still serviceable, chassis with new wooden bodywork.

The last three paragraphs appeared on another page of the magazine and they conclude the editorial as follows:

(veneered) hardboard may be used as a substitute where necessary on the framing. The section in Fig. 6 shows how the panelling is secured by fillets screwed to rails and pillars. A fair clearance between edges of panelling and

above lower edge of chassis as the bulge of axle case above the rest of axle.

Whilst on this subject the question of clearance between the rear wheel and its housing must also be considered. In the case of an "articulated bump" (where one wheel remains on level ground whilst the other goes over a bump) the wheel moves inwards as well as upwards, and the width of wheel housing must therefore allow for this. Assuming Fig. 4 to be drawn to scale, the sideways clearance is calculated by placing a piece of tracing paper over the drawing and tracing in wheels and axle. Pin tracing paper to drawing at point (B), then swing paper round so that wheels and axle move just as they would in an articulated bump. When axle reaches position shown by dotted lines (axle touching chassis) this may be taken as the maximum articulated bump, and the new position of wheel then traced on to original drawing. The wheel housing must now be built to take this extreme wheel position, side rail (H, Fig. 1) being taken inwards if necessary by slanting the rising member (G) slightly away from the wheel. In making the scale drawing for these calculations it must be remembered that a chassis goes down on its springs 3 in. to 4 in. when the body, passengers, luggage, etc., are in position, and it is this chassis position which has to be drawn to scale. An extra clearance of 1 in. to 1½ in. should also be allowed for the use of chains on tyres.

Bottom Frame.—Details of this are given in Figs. 1 and 3. The rising members (G) are checked slightly into the side members and secured with screws, as shown in Fig. 3. At their top ends they join the rear side members (H) as shown in Fig. 1, also screwed. (P) is checked slightly into the rear corner pillars and screwed home.

Side Frames.—Reference to Fig. 1 will give a good idea of the side frame construction, doors being shown in position, but with lower intermediate rails missing, since these are applied afterwards outside the panelling. The pillars (coachbuilding term for stiles) of doors and body framing are curved on the outside, thus giving the "tumble-in" and "turn-under" (see section Fig. 6). On the inside, however, they have two straight surfaces at an angle to each other, as shown, with the exception of the rear corner pillars, which are shaped as in rear view (Fig. 5). Rebates for panelling on these rear pillars, however, must line up with those of the other pillars. Owing to the angle at which Fig. 1 is presented, it is not noticeable that the front or "screen" pillars also have their "tumble-in" and "turn-under," a point which must be borne in mind when marking out. The

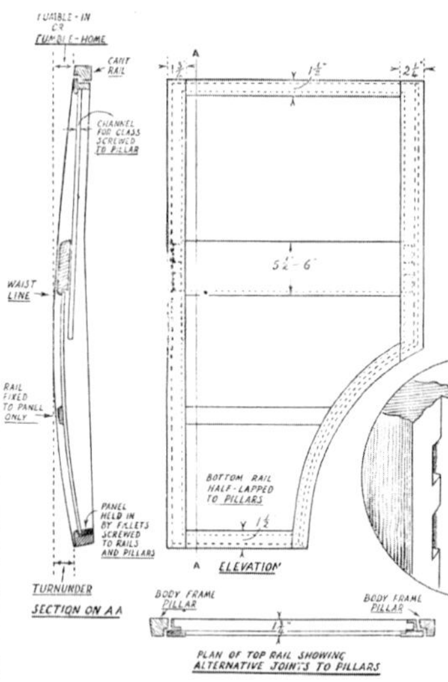

FIG. 6. DOOR CONSTRUCTION

Curvature of doors ("Tumble-in" and "Turn-under") may lead to fouling at top and bottom as doors are opened and closed. This problem will be dealt with in the second half of the article in our next issue.

INSET: How waist rail is tenoned into door pillar (inside view). Tenons are secured with oak pegs let in from inside surface of pillar. Rear waist rail of car body is tenoned in same way, but must also be rebated at rear of top edge, to take rear upper plywood panel (FIG. 1)

external curvature unfortunately complicates hingeing of doors, and this will be dealt with later in the article.

The wide centre rails or "waist rails" of doors and body framing are double tenoned into the pillars as shown in Fig. 6 (inset) and oak pegs driven through the tenons from the inside face of the pillars. The top rail or "cant rail" (Fig. 1) is made in two pieces joined with a scarf joint, and the front and rear pillars are stub-tenoned into it, then secured by screwing through from the top. These two joints are complicated by cross rails joining the tops of the side frames at front and rear, details of which will be given in next month's issue.

The cant rail itself is curved slightly in elevation as well as in plan. The intermediate pillars (K and L) are through-tenoned to the cant rail, and pinned. Rear quarter rail (N) is tenoned into (L) and the rear corner pillar, the cant rail being screwed down to (N). (M) and (O) may be in one piece halved to the cant rail, waist rail and wheel arch, where it should be flush on the inside. The outer face of (O) is set back so as to come inside the panelling.

All rails should be set back slightly, say ¹⁄₁₆ in. to ⅛ in., from the face of the pillars. This "breaks the joint," and if any discrepancy occurs in this distance, it does not show up so badly as if the surfaces were obviously intended to be flush, but did not remain so.

Rebates to take ¼ in. Gaboon-faced ply panelling

(Continued on page 63)

… large centre panel extending between the auxiliary roof rails and the two side pieces which cover the metal corner panels. These are stitched together, tacked to the cant rails and fixed to the side corner panels with rubber solution.

At the front and rear roof sticks, the leather cloth is butted against the metal head panels, the joints being finished by a moulding (see section DD). Along the cant rails, a cornice is screwed down over the leather cloth. The function of the cornice is to drain away water as it comes off the roof. For this reason, it follows the curve of the cant rail, sloping downwards towards front and back. At the front it is carried on down the screen pillar, as in Fig. 2, and at the back it is carried round to the other side, as in Fig. 5, where alternative shapes for the cornice are shown.

A metal cornice would be shaped as indicated, and is obtainable in lengths drilled for screwing. If made from wood, it must be given the alternative shape shown in Fig. 5.

Sectional dimensions for roof framing (*see* Fig. 10):

Intermediate roof sticks 1⅜in by ⅞in

Front and rear roof sticks 1⅜in by 1³⁄₁₆in

Front slats 1⅜in by ⁵⁄₁₆in

Auxiliary roof rails 1¼in by 1¼in

SHOOTING BRAKE
HOW TO CONVERT YOUR CAR (*Continued from last month*)

In the first part of this article the use of synthetic resin glue was mentioned. The following may also be used as alternatives, however ; White lead mixed to a paste with raw linseed oil (if coachwork is to have a painted finish). If a varnish finish is contemplated, joints should be put together with gold size or varnish. Screws should also be employed wherever possible, to reinforce joints, and put in with tallow to prevent rusting. For a good finish, they should also be well countersunk and hidden where necessary with stopping coloured to match the timber

Wheel Housing.—Fig. 9 gives constructional details of the wheel housing, elm being used if possible for the inside wall, as this timber is resistant to damp.

Doors.—These have already been partly dealt with, Fig. 6 showing their construction. The windows are arranged to move vertically in glass channelling screwed to the pillars, or are made to slide horizontally in two pieces, the channelling being screwed to top and waist rails. The latter is the better method for the front door window, owing to its shape.

The external curvature unfortunately complicates hingeing and calculation of the " shut bevel " on the pillars. Fig. 8 (X) shows how an average " shut bevel " results in fouling of the door at top or bottom if too much " tumble-in " or " turn-under " is adopted, whilst Fig. 8 (Y), drawn to scale, shows a normal " tumble-in " and " turn-under," thus avoiding fouling with an average shut bevel.

To determine the exact amount of shut bevel required, a plan view of doors and corresponding pillars of body frame should be drawn to scale, showing sections through all pillars at waistline and extreme top and bottom, as in Fig. 8 (Y). Hinge positions (hinges standing slightly proud of waistline) should next be marked in. If doors are hinged, as in Fig. 2, the section through pillars at top of front door and bottom of rear door will come correspondingly nearer to hinges, and must be positioned accurately in the drawing, thus giving three shut pillar positions for each door.

By striking arcs from the hinge position on each door, the path of the " shut pillar " as the door is opened may be traced at all these points. The amount of " shut bevel " required to avoid fouling is thus ascertained.

Rear.—Fig. 5 shows how the rear tail-boards are hinged. Rail (F) should be placed so that the bottom tail-board is level with the rear floor when opened.

The tail-boards themselves have the usual mortise and tenon framed construction with rebates to take ½ in. gaboon-faced ply panelling, which comes flush on

the inside, as in Fig. 1 (Section AB) so that when the lower tail-board is dropped, a level surface is presented for use. Top tail-board should be fitted with metal stays for support when opened, whilst bottom tail-board should have hooks and chains to take any considerable weight.

Front.—Fig. 7 shows how the metal " scuttle panel " extends to cover the screen pillars and is pinned into the windscreen rebate. It is also pinned into the door rebates of the screen pillars.

The existing scuttle panel could probably be adapted to the new body, and in some cases the whole of the original screen pillar might be left intact and incorporated in the new body, thus obviating any difficulties with the scuttle panel.

Flooring.—This should be of ½ in. plywood (or any of the ply substitutes available) fitted with rebates of bottom frame, and screwed down where convenient. Flooring at the front should be sloped as shown by dotted lines in Fig. 2.

Seats.—In most cases, existing seats can be adapted to the new body. Front seats are usually of the " bucket " type and the adjustable floor fixing is easily transferred to a new floor.

Roof.—Fig. 7 shows how the screen pillars are connected by a head rail, and the arrangement of the corner joints involved. A rear head rail connects the rear corner pillars in the same way, a similar joint being used.

Fig. 10 shows the roof construction, which consists of " roof sticks " joining the two side frames together at intervals. About six of these should be used. Slats (usually of pine) run lengthwise and about 2 in. to 2½ in. apart across the top of the intermediate roof sticks, but are lapped to the end roof sticks as shown. An auxiliary roof rail runs parallel with the slats at each side, and is halved to all roof sticks, care being taken not to weaken the latter at the halving joint (joint should go no further than approximately ⅓ of the depth of the roof sticks).

When the roof framing is complete, it is screwed to the cant rails, and curved metal panels are fixed at front, back and sides, these being pinned or screwed to front and rear roof sticks (see section DD, Fig. 10), also to rebates in auxiliary roof rails and cant rails (see section CC, Fig. 10). Front head panel and side corner panels could in many cases be taken from the original roof, but it is doubtful whether the original rear head panel could be used, since its curvature is likely to be unsuitable for a shooting brake body.

For the roof covering, two layers of leather cloth are used, a stuffing of cotton wool being placed between them. The bottom layer lies face downwards. Both layers extend from front roof stick to rear roof stick (see section DD, Fig. 10). The bottom layer, extends across the body as far as the auxiliary roof rails to which it is tacked (see section CC, Fig. 10). The upper layer lies face upwards and is made in three pieces ; one

(*Continued on page 73*)

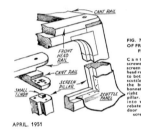

FIG. 7. DETAIL OF FRAMING AT FRONT

Cant rail is screwed down to screen pillar, then head rail is screwed to both. A metal scuttle panel joins the body to the bonnet and runs right up screen pillar. It is pinned into windscreen rebate, also into door rebate of screen pillar

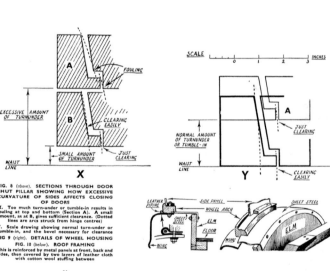

FIG. 8 (*above*). SECTIONS THROUGH DOOR SHUT PILLAR SHOWING HOW EXCESSIVE CURVATURE OF SIDES AFFECTS CLOSING OF DOORS

X. Too much turn-under or tumble-in results in fouling at top and bottom (Section A). A small amount, as at B, gives sufficient clearance. (Dotted lines are arcs struck from hinge centres)

Y. Scale drawing showing normal turn-under or tumble-in, and the bevel necessary for clearance

FIG 9 (*right*). DETAILS OF WHEEL HOUSING

FIG. 10 (*below*). ROOF FRAMING

This is reinforced by metal panels at front, back and sides, then covered by two layers of leather cloth with cotton wool stuffing between

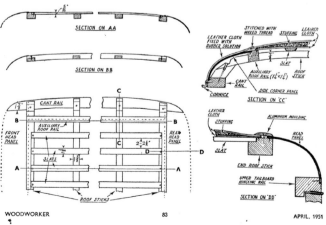

107

CHAPTER 13

How to Build Light Vans, Trucks and Buses

The commercial vehicle and public service vehicle industry was a heavy user of wood-framed vehicle bodies and cabs yet is one restoration sector that is often overlooked today. So I have made a special point of including a section on the techniques used on such vehicles, as there are many interesting facets that we can all learn from.

There's a lot of theory in coachbuilding, some of which translates to an actual rebuild, but there is much that doesn't. One of the theories is that small panel vans have to be the simplest of all wooden-framed vehicles to restore as the small size, general box-like structure and lack of numerous complicated doors means they should be really easy to rebuild. Well, try telling that to somebody who has restored one.

Wood framing was the material of choice for specialist body builders and low volume manufacturers, such as can be seen in this 1930s Morris truck.

Commercial vehicle bodies of all types used wooden framing until well into the 1950s.

A typical such van is the 1939 Bedford BYC 12cwt delivery van, which, at the time of writing, has just had a new body frame built by Peter Delicata, a commercial motor body builder from Staffordshire, England. Peter acquired the van from a Vauxhall collector who wanted a commercial vehicle, but not a huge truck, which would create storage problems.

Peter's experience probably echoes that of most people who restore vintage CVs in that, unlike cars of the same period, there are usually no drawings or parts available for commercials. So you have to learn to be creative!

Fortunately Peter had years of experience in the vehicle body-building industry to draw on and the resources of a professional workshop. As a result, the quality of the workmanship is outstanding, and the images highlight the attention to detail that all would-be restorers could learn from.

Wood framing allowed vehicle manufacturers and body builders alike the freedom to adapt a van's size and specification to meet a customer's exact requirements.

Unitary construction of buses was still a rarity in the 1950s, and so London Transport took delivery of more than 6,000 double-deckers that used both wood and metal in the construction of their bodywork.

Wooden truck cabs were popular in Europe right up to the 1950s and should prove no more difficult to rebuild than a typical coachbuilt car.

The bodywork on this Leyland Tiger bus highlights some of the design features available to coachbuilding firms when using wooden framework.

The 1939 Bedford van couldn't be further from the perception that all early vans are just boxes on wheels. Peter Delicata has gone to great lengths to cut and shape the ash to retain the gentle curves of the original design.

Note how the uprights curve in at the bottom to mirror the curvature of the steel bulkhead. It would be all too easy to make the uprights completely straight if you really want that boxy look.

This shows how the inward curved bottom of the rear uprights has been formed from three pieces of ash that have been glued and bolted together using a steel plate for strength.

Even the roof is curved from front to back, but it also curves inwards at the front over the driver's compartment. This has been achieved using more than one piece of wood to maintain strength whilst allowing for the correct curvature to be achieved.

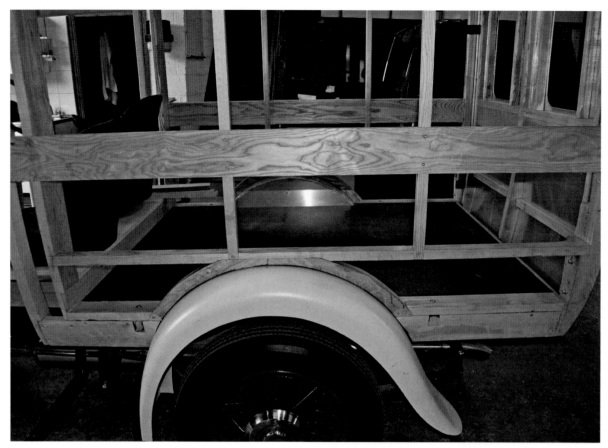

This shot not only highlights how the sections of the framework are screwed together, but it also shows the extra horizontal rail between the waist level frame and the sill section. This extra horizontal rail provides extra strength and rigidity and a firm base for the side uprights to anchor to.

This shot shows how the waist rail has been rebated into the uprights to create a smooth and uncluttered finish. Note the slight step up into the passenger compartment and the steel plates that add strength to the rear lower corners – you wouldn't expect to see these plates exposed on a car, but it is perfectly acceptable on a commercial vehicle.

RIGHT: *Even the rear doors curve in at the bottom. Note how the aluminium panelling has been cut along the folded edge to allow the panel to follow the curve of the wood.*

Note how the rear hinges are recessed into both the rear upright and the door frame itself. These hinges were purchased as blanks and had to be drilled and cut to length.

Whilst the inside of vans was not usually panelled, the rear doors often were, with either plywood or metal. Note how Peter has rebated the bottom door rail to allow the inside panel to fit flush. Nice touch!

Joints like these wouldn't work on a station wagon with an exposed frame, but they are fine for a vehicle that will have its exterior frame panelled over. Just make sure the screws are countersunk to avoid them rubbing on the exterior panels.

BELOW: This shot shows how the curvature of the wooden frame will be complemented by the exterior panelling.

Many truck manufacturers across Europe were using wood-framed cabs right up to the 1950s, while wooden truck bodies were still being built into the 1970s. In fact many body build-ers also incorporated wooden-framed cabs into box van bodies into the 1970s as well.

Although often simple in design and construction, truck cabs and bodies tend to be built from heavier gauge materials in order to better withstand the usage and load factors that trucks have to endure during their working lives.

This Dennis truck cab is framed entirely from wood and highlights that although it is a relatively small structure, the thickness of the material used and the number of vertical and horizontal supports show that it was built to take the punishment that trucks receive during their working lives.

The roof section and the rear cab panelling had been stripped off so that work could proceed on moving the rear of the cab back by 6–8in (10–14cm) to provide more space inside the cab without detracting from its overall appearance or visual dimensions.

Here we see that the doors, roof and cab floor have been removed, and the rear section has been clamped in place further back to allow for new sections to be put in.

Moving back the rear section of the cab necessitated making longer roof supports with a new curvature.

This shows that although the original door capping could be retained in order to preserve the shape of the original door opening, it had to be spliced into a new door top frame in order to match the new roof curvature.

Almost finished! What appeared to be a simple job also involved building part of a new base for the seats, and new, longer step/floor sections.

New rear aluminium panels finish off the job to a professional standard.

TOP: This 1943 ex-Westmorland Fire Brigade Dodge water tender arrived at the workshops of Rusty Trucks restoration services in Cumbria in a derelict condition.

MIDDLE: The large crew cab area is accessed by sliding doors, and this proved very time-consuming to get right.

BOTTOM: The side locker doors were amongst the few original parts salvageable, and so the truck required a completely new body built to the original design and construction method and assembled using birch plywood.

Work inside the crew cab involved building storage lockers and seat frames as well as the basic structure.

Once the body structure was finished it was clad in aluminium, and of course painted fire engine red!

Whilst wood framing was commonly used on bus and coach bodies well into the 1950s, it is unusual to see it used externally, as on this Ford.

ABOVE: The wood framing on this Gilford bus had suffered many sub-standard repair jobs previously and will require an almost entirely new body at Historic Vehicle Restoration.

RIGHT: Although it looks as if little remains of the original bodywork on this Leyland Lion bus, 95 per cent of the old timber work was saved to allow accurate patterns to be made.

It would easy to build a completely new body, but the cab and bulkhead of this Leyland Lion will be retained and incorporated into the new structure in order to try to keep as much of the original structure as possible.

New bodywork being built from the ground up around the original cab structure.

BELOW: *The new floor structure is built by Historic Vehicle Restorations from seasoned oak following traditional coachbuilding techniques.*

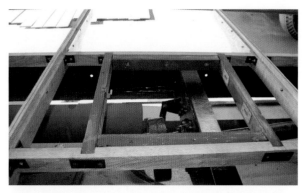

The original oak structure around the rear has been left in place not only to act as a reference point for the next floor sections, but also because it was good enough to reuse.

The original frame for this inspection hatch was deemed to be in good shape so has been retained. In addition, all the original brackets have been reused.

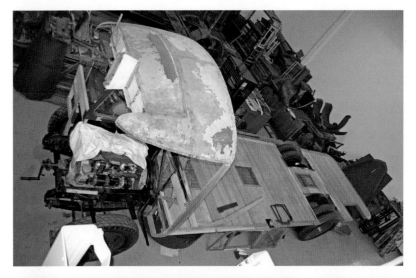

LEFT: The new floor will provide an excellent base on which to construct a new body frame. Siberian larch has been used instead of Douglas fir, as the latter is becoming increasingly difficult to source in good quality, slow-grown varieties.

BELOW: New wood on the left side of the front bulkhead blends in with the original wood being retained on the right side.

The original rear entrance partition will obviously need some major work!

The new front bulkhead pillars are substantial components and have been cut from a single piece of 2in- (5cm-) thick ash.

New ash framing was spliced into the existing bulkhead to form a strong structure.

Once the original cab and bulkhead had been supported and a new floor laid, construction of the new bodywork could commence.

With new pillars in place, the bodywork of the old Leyland starts to take shape.

The new pillars are attached to the floor with metal flitch/gusset plates.

The pillars are an exact copy of the lines of the original that curve inwards below the floor level, giving an aesthetic 'turn-under' in coachbuilding terms.

The waist rail seen here is clamped in place to help support the uprights and hold them squarely in place while the fit-out takes place.

The new larchwood floor will eventually be covered in period flooring material – a traditional linoleum. Here we see some sample material.

Even at this 'skeleton' stage the old Leyland is starting to look like a bus again.

Additional side rails provide both additional rigidity and support for external panels.

The pillars also have additional metal bracing plates to give support below the floor.

Internally the pillars are tied into the outriggers by triangulated gusset plates replicating the original body-builder's design.

The pillars also have a metal flitch plate running through the centre to give extra strength. They are secured by means of a CSK slotted bolt and a similar nut known as a 'Weymann nut' after its inventor Charles Weymann of Weymann Motor Bodies.

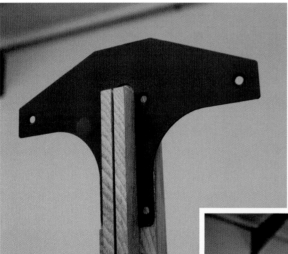

ABOVE: The top of the pillars will be bolted to the side cant rails via copies of the original steel gusset plates.

BELOW: Externally the waist rails are scalloped around each window frame.

The front metal panelwork is recessed into the wooden frame. All external side panels will be rebated in the same way.

The original metal side panels were in good shape and will be reused. Here we see a trial fit.

The rear metal roof section of the Leyland is being repaired and will be incorporated into the new bodywork. It also provided useful data location and the shape of the rear section of the body.

The original side panels fit neatly into a rebate under the waist rails.

The original rear framework pieces are in good enough shape from which to make new pattern parts.

The old Leyland is really starting to look like a bus again…

This Bedford OB bus was delivered new to Bristol Tramways in 1949 and was acquired by Mike Walker in 2009.

ABOVE: The Duple body is seen here being stripped of its metal panels so that the extent of any damage to the underlying wooden framework can be revealed.

New uprights have been inserted on the left rear side and given a protective coat of grey paint.

Most of the major repairs were confined to the rear of the Duple bodywork, as indicated by the grey-painted woodwork.

The newly panelled and painted bus stands outside the TDC workshops.

CHAPTER 14

How to Build Newbuilds and Phantoms

As classic wooden-bodied vehicles have increased in popularity, and value, in recent years, so demand for affordable examples has facilitated a growth in the number of newbuilds. In the USA such vehicles are often referred to as 'phantoms', a term that by its own definition implies something which is pretending to be something that it's not. Maybe if somebody takes the chassis and cowl from a 1946 Ford woodie and builds their own station wagon body, then that could loosely be described as a phantom. On the other hand, if somebody takes a derelict chassis from say a 1934 Buick, 1937 Rolls-Royce or 1947 Austin and builds their own wooden

station wagon body on it, then how can it be a phantom, when it's not pretending to be a woodie … it really is one!

Here in the UK we refer to such vehicles as 'newbuilds', as each is unique in its own right, and we embrace the skill, enthusiasm and hard work that goes into creating such a vehicle. So for the rest of this chapter I shall use the term newbuild out of respect for the people who create these interesting and unique machines.

The 1930s and 1940s saw the creation of some truly stylish automobiles with both steel- and wood-framed bodywork mounted on substantial chassis. Whilst the ravages of time, weather and

poor storage may have reduced some surviving examples to little more than a rusting hulk, there are those amongst us who, fortunately, can visualize that resurrecting this junk pile into a beautiful wood-framed panel van, station wagon or convertible is a project they can handle.

At the outbreak of hostilities in Europe in 1939 large numbers of unsold North American and British cars and light commercials were requisitioned by the British Government's war department and hastily re-bodied as ambulances, fire trucks, food wagons and recovery vehicles. At the end of World War II these modified vehicles

Webster's Encyclopaedic Dictionary *states that a phantom (a commonly used phrase in the USA) is 'something which is only apparently what it purports to be' – which seems to belittle all the hard work that restorers and vehicle builders put into creating a vehicle that is clearly exactly what it purports to be!*

Newbuilds can take on all forms from outlandish designs to exact nut and bolt replicas of an original design.

If you are really lucky you might be able to purchase a wooden body that somebody else has discarded, but don't hold your breath.

were the first to be disposed of, and most saw service with new bodywork on the rear.

Today, such vehicles sometimes appear as barn finds, but a 1938 Packard tow truck with a rusty crane on the back is hardly a promising restoration project. However, re-bodying such a vehicle as a roadster or woodie wagon is much more appealing and worthwhile.

At the other end of the scale, not everybody wants or can afford a beautifully restored or original wood-framed vehicle, and may want to create their own, perhaps combining their own bodyworking skills with the remains of a vehicle lying in a friend's garage, or found at the local junk yard or maybe on an online auction site.

Here in the UK we have a rich history of hundreds of small coachbuilding firms constructing vehicle bodies on just about every conceivable chassis make and type. As chairman of the Woodie Car Club I am often contacted by enthusiasts who have found a chassis/cowl of one of their favourite manufacturers, and wonder whether anybody had previously bodied such a vehicle as a woodie wagon because it could inspire them to do the same.

At the time of writing we have club members across the UK and Europe designing and constructing newbuild woodie wagons on chassis ranging from Armstrong Siddeley and Daimler to MG and Sunbeam Talbot. I've also seen a number of such potential restorers decide that newbuilding a wagon body might be beyond their skills, so

Small vans are popular newbuild vehicles.

This wood-framed newbuild Austin 10 van even incorporates the car's original rear side windows in its rear doors.

This unique Jaguar Foxbat was constructed in the 1970s from the derelict remains of a Jaguar XK150 and a Morris Minor Traveller so that the owner could transport his dogs.

Quite why anybody would want to take the trouble to graft the rear end of a Morris Minor Traveller on to a four-door sedan when there are literally thousands of Travellers available for sale is beyond this writer... but this photo shows what can be done.

This MG converted to a wooden-bodied utility during World War II may be long gone, but a newbuild version is now taking shape in Holland.

were clamped to the chassis and cowl. Once the basic visual effects, proportions and contours were satisfactory, thoughts were given to the engineering. For example, will the doors swing into the opening with the given hinge offset? The engineering needs to be planned well in advance of the actual build to eliminate potential problems. Grant tells us:

> One of the biggest problems with any project is that you are going where nobody has been before. Also you have to work out the best way to join parts from one vehicle to another. I lengthened the floorpan of the S10 and had much fun mating it to the firewall/bulkhead of the Morris.
>
> Being of all wood construction, the front doors created some hingeing problems, and I had to cut the 'cups' off the Morris's steel front doors and rework them to fit the wood frames. I then had to extend the trailing edges of the front wings/fenders to align with these.

As a general rule it seems that the average newbuild project starts life following the acquisition of a vehicle with tired or missing bodywork. Some do start with just an idea to construct a newbuild, but either way the real starting point with any newbuild project is with a way to visualize the concept.

have opted to build a panel van body instead.

Newbuilds are created for a variety of reasons, and perhaps one of the most common thought processes is to create a vehicle that has the charm and style of something old, but is coupled with a modern drive-train to give it more drivability. This was exactly the reasoning behind the unique 'MOS10' woodie completed by Canadian Grant Rae, in 2007.

Grant had already honed his coach-building skills during 3,000 hours, spread over nine years, restoring a 1946 Pontiac Deluxe woodie, but when he stumbled across a rusty Morris MO Oxford sedan, an idea for another woodie project was born. Grant had always had a soft spot for the Morris Minor, but being over 6ft 4in tall he had to discount the possibility of ever owning one. However, the MO Oxford was the Minor's big brother, and Grant knew he had to have it.

After measuring the front end sheet metal of the Morris and comparing it with the dimensions of a Chevrolet S10 pick-up truck chassis, a design evolved. The patterns and lines of the Pontiac woodie provided the inspiration for a two-door, ash-framed and mahogany-panelled woodie.

The wood-framing measurements were drawn up full scale on cardboard and 8 × 4 sheets of plywood, which

Canadian Grant Rae's newbuild woodie, known as MOS10, which combined the front sheet metal from a Morris Oxford MO-series sedan with a Chevy S10 pick-up running gear, sports styling cues taken from Grant's Pontiac woodie.

LEFT: Getting the initial design right. Try photocopying a brochure and sketching on the design for your wooden bodywork.

BELOW: This image of a 1930s Ford 10HP converted to a shooting brake clearly demonstrates where design took preference over function. This was a small car to start with, but it beats me how anybody could squeeze in through those front doors! There's a lesson here.

If you have the model-making skills, one possible route is to build a model of the proposed vehicle, perhaps using one of the many $\frac{1}{43}$rd, $\frac{1}{32}$nd, $\frac{1}{25}$th or even $\frac{1}{18}$th scale proprietary models currently available as a base. Another method is to make some sketches or drawings, whilst a third option is to follow the lead of Hugh Nutting from Kalispell, Montana, who cleverly used brochure cut-outs when visualizing his 1939 LaSalle woodie wagon.

Hugh found that the Buick 40 series shared the same cowl and floorpan as the LaSalle, and with other similarities between Oldsmobile and Pontiac he was able to draw the body from an Olds woodie on to a brochure photocopy of the LaSalle sheet metal to create a picture-perfect visual.

SIZE, TYPE AND DESIGN

Two doors or four; tailgate or rear doors; fixed or wind-up windows; wood or metal roof? Are you going to remove the entire rear section of an existing body; will it have a metal or wooden floor; how much of the existing cowl (assuming there is one) and windscreen/windshield surround can be retained? These are just some of the many questions that you need to ask yourself before going beyond the initial design stage.

Some people have been a little gung-ho in the past with the cutting, sawing and removal of vehicle bodywork and have not given enough thought to how the basic structure of the new bodywork might look on their chosen chassis. The sensible approach is to build full-size templates out of cheap sheets of plywood, hardboard or MDF, and these can be clamped on to the vehicle chassis so that the lines of how the finished vehicle might look can be visualized.

With surprisingly few woodie wagons ever making it 'down under', and those that did being pounded into splinters on tough Australian outback roads, John Knight from Queensland faced quite a task when he decided to turn a 1937 Buick, originally purchased as a parts car, into a woodie wagon. Despite handing the construction of the timber framing over to a local boat builder, John still had to come up with a design for the newbuild.

Making full size templates out of plywood, fibreboard, MDF or even cardboard will help you get the lines and proportions right for the size and style of your chosen chassis.

As no photographs of original 1937 Buick woodies could be found, John and his wife Ruth settled on taking design cues from a 1946 Ford, and these were transferred on to sheets of $\frac{3}{8}$in MDF, which were clamped to the Buick's frame. Apparently the basic outline was drawn at least five times before everybody settled on a shape that 'looked right'.

I'd suggest studying the lines and dimensions of photos of similar-sized vehicles and, if possible, check the shapes and angles of similar surviving vehicles – ask their owners if you can measure the key dimensions, especially the height over the length of body.

Whilst it may seem easy to use straight lengths when constructing a new frame, it must be remembered that the most visually pleasing designs are full of curves and angles. By using full-size templates you can see how those curves could translate into an appealing vehicle design, and you'll be able to start working out shapes and angles before you ever take your expensive hardwood anywhere near a saw.

Newbuilds don't have to conform to any styling cues that have gone before and you are basically free to create a design that suits your tastes and requirements.

The designer of the replica 1940 Willys went for a reverse curve at the rear, which probably makes it unique amongst wooden-bodied station wagons.

Once you've worked out the general shape, lines and proportions, you can then start thinking about where the various pieces of framework will go. You'll also need to give some thought to areas such as how the wooden frame will attach to the chassis, and will the doors be hung on forward or rear pillars (suicide fashion), and will the pillars be of sufficient strength to take the weight of the doors?

In addition, you'll need to think about how you'll attach the rear wings, plywood panels and windows (assuming there are any). Going through this process and identifying problems and solutions long before you cut the first piece of wood will not only save you much time, but also frustration and money later in the project.

I can recall exchanging emails with a man who was about to disassemble a coachbuilt Rolls-Royce hearse and rebuild it as a woodie station wagon. He had already found a number of photos of similar original vehicles, and I sent him a number of detailed images of an Austin woodie wagon I was restoring at the time. So I was surprised when I arranged to visit him and view the project to see a pile of discarded, and expensive, ash piled up in the corner.

When questioned about the discarded timber he said that he had missed a crucial point, evident in all the photos, which was that on most coachbuilt woodie wagons the front and last support pillars are generally the same height, giving the vehicle a balanced and symmetrical appearance. So he had initially constructed the rear of his wagon with a distinct slope towards the rear, and it was only when he took a good look at the images I had sent him, and he stood back and looked at his newbuild, that he realized his error. Still, it was nothing that several more days work and new wood to the value

A newbuild allows you to be creative not only as to how many doors you want, but whether they are forward or rear hinged.

of a few hundred pounds couldn't put right.

As a general rule older car bodies have a barrel shape, in that the roof line curves up slightly in the middle and the sides usually bow out slightly at the B-pillar. Using timber that is dead straight means your newbuild really could end up looking like a proverbial 'shed on wheels'.

One of the advantages of a newbuild vehicle is that you will definitely end up with something that is unique. It may look like something that went before, but you'll be able to incorporate styling cues and equipment that suits your personal taste. If you are really tall, for instance, you can increase the roof height so that you won't have to duck whenever you get in and out, and you can increase the length of the front doors so that you don't have to squeeze in behind the wheel.

A newbuild allows you to maximize your creative skills both on the outside and the inside. On the inside you may wish to use stock front seats that are appropriate to the chassis make and model, but the rear seats (if there are to be any) may need you to be a little more creative. You may choose to give the finished body to an interior trimmer and let them build a new rear seat, or you may acquire such a seat from a junk yard or vehicle dismantler and craft the vehicle's rear bodywork around it.

If you are building a vehicle with just two front doors you'll need to think about whether you need access to the rear. It's not a good idea to have fixed front seats if rear passengers have to climb over them to get in. Bus seats are not only for buses, but can also be used in the rear of shooting brakes/woodies and even panel vans, and can often be picked up cheaply from commercial vehicle dismantlers.

Another area where a little foresight can pay dividends is with bodywork hardware, such as locks, hinges, door handles, window mechanisms and so on. You can source most of these parts from specialist suppliers or even junk yards ahead of the build, but even having an idea of the parts you'll be using could stop you making the costly mistake of cutting and shaping expensive hardwoods only to find out later on in the build that the hardware won't fit as planned and you've got to start tearing things apart.

I recently came across a restorer who had made a brilliant job of converting steel car doors into a fabulous half-timbered style. However, it was only after all his hard work that he realized he could no longer fit the window mechanisms and would now have to drive the car without any front windows!

In the USA the popularity of the wooden-bodied station wagon has seen an acute shortage of viable restoration projects. The vast size of the country, along with different geography and weather patterns, often means that many 'project' cars have suffered from the dreaded ravages of the rust bug. Whilst the wooden bodywork can be remade, the biggest obstruction to returning these vehicles to the highway often lies with seriously corroded metal floors and front cowls/bulkheads.

To counter this problem a number of suppliers are now producing replacement cowls and floors out of fibreglass, and some of the best I've seen are being sold by Eric Johnson at Treehouse Woods in Florida. Using aircraft-grade glass fibre, reinforced with steel inserts, these replica Ford panels are not only in increasing demand by woodie wagon restorers but are also proving popular with those wishing to construct a newbuild/phantom woodie using a sedan chassis. Eric comments:

If you are building a vehicle with just two front doors you'll need to think about whether you need access to the rear. It's not a good idea to have fixed front seats if rear passengers have to climb over them to get in. This Riley in Australia clearly had room for rear doors but they were omitted during the build. It must be a real squeeze getting into the rear seats!

Original Ford cowls are now very rare and very expensive. If you can find one they are often rotted out, and being double skinned in places they are very difficult to repair to a high standard. Woodies are all about visual appearance, and with most of the cowl exposed when you open the hood, a perfect cowl portrays the right image. Restoring a woodie wagon or constructing a newbuild vehicle is expensive, and when you put that much money into a car you want it to be perfect.

ABOVE: Not strictly a newbuild, but definitely not a standard production vehicle, as this three-door Morris Minor Traveller was built new in this configuration using a van chassis.

LEFT: However, this shows you what you could do...anybody fancy a four-door Traveller?

ABOVE: This shot shows a mock-up hinge arrangement – note the use of a steel B-pillar to provide added strength and rigidity.

RIGHT: Eric Johnson from Treehouse Woodies in Florida has overcome the shortage of sound original steel Ford cowls by producing replicas in aircraft-grade fibreglass reinforced with steel. They are ideal for restoring original Ford woodies, and can also be used to create newbuild/phantoms.

Be prepared to make things fit around the bodywork you are creating. You may well find that standard running boards won't fit your newbuild, so why not custom make them from exterior grade plywood?

Installing wind-up windows in a newbuild door needs careful planning to get all the angles and dimensions correct. Many newbuilders simply opt for sliding glass instead.

ABOVE: Don't forget somewhere to place the spare wheel. Many woodies had the spare hanging outside on the rear tailgate, but make sure the wooden frame and the bracketry is strong enough to carry the weight.

RIGHT: If hanging the spare wheel on the rear tailgate you will need to be precise with its location: too high and it will foul the top tailgate, too low and it will hit the bottom panel. You may need to recess the bottom panel to stop the wheel fouling the bodywork when the bottom tailgate is lowered.

ABOVE: If the rear of the vehicle is being designed to carry goods or luggage (even if in reality nothing will ever be placed there), an industrial floor covering can make a great alternative to bare wood or carpet.

RIGHT: Newbuilds offer a great deal of choice for the selection of front seats. However, rear seats rarely just slot right in, and you may have to adapt the rear floor of the vehicle to suit the seats, rather than the other way around.

Brian Glass from Queensland, Australia, acquired a unique Australian-bodied 1946 Plymouth woodie. While not a phantom or a newbuild, by any stretch of the imagination, Brian's interesting interior roof modification could certainly be great for any newbuilder. It turned out the car had a steel roof mounted on timber cross-members, which was originally clad with plywood sheets. So Brian decided to reverse engineer a strip-wood interior roof using locally sourced Australian mountain ash (Eucalyptus regans).

The roof interior is now starting to look like an original factory job.

Varnishing really brings out the colour of the wood.

'HEY MISTER, DOES THAT CAR FLOAT?'

Of course, not all newbuilds are sedans or woodies. When Mike Gilroy wanted something special to add to his fleet of wedding cars he naturally chose a Rolls-Royce and ended up acquiring a 1934 20/25HP model that had originally been a limousine until somebody had decided to hack the roof off. This effectively gave Mike a clean sheet to start with, and so after completely overhauling the chassis and mechanicals, he started on a ten-year project to build a boat-tail body.

Mike tells us that he knew the new body would be lighter than the one he was replacing, so he decided to construct the new body to be as strong as possible, including a number of metal brackets for added strength and rigidity.

Here we can see the rough shape and dimensions being laid out.

And here's the completed bodyshell.

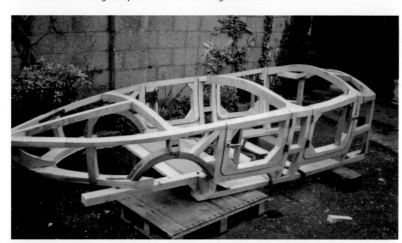

Boat-tail convertibles are proving a popular method of to convert a derelict chassis into a truly eye-catching and practical vehicle.

TOP LEFT: *An engine hoist was used to lower the new wooden frame on to the chassis.*

TOP RIGHT: *Mike decided to over-engineer the joints to help add strength and rigidity to the body frame.*

ABOVE & RIGHT: *The boat-tail and front bulkhead were covered in alternating teak and mahogany strips, with thin spacer strips between each strip.*

When all the strips were firmly glued, they were then planed flat and sanded smooth.

The end result is stunning.

The front bulkhead looks equally glorious with the teak and mahogany strips.

CHAPTER 15

Colouring and Varnishing

So the woodwork is stripped, shaped, bleached and sanded, and now you've arrived at the really important process – applying the finish. If your wood-framed vehicle is going to have an exposed exterior then you'll need to give much more thought to the finish than you would if all your hard work were ultimately panelled over.

Choosing the right finish for your woodwork depends on several important considerations: is the wood being restored to its original condition, and how much of it will be on show? Will the vehicle be shown and judged for points on its originality? Will it be a 'garage queen' and used exclusively for shows and events, or will it perhaps be your 'daily driver'?

Do you live in a cold, damp climate, or maybe a desert region? Or perhaps near the ocean where the air is salty?

Do you like a super shiny finish on the wood? Do you have access to spraying facilities? Do you have a vision for how the finished woodwork will look?

The list of questions is almost endless, but the answers can dictate the type, quality and longevity of the resulting finish. Wood can become a thing of beauty and an 'attention magnet' at shows and displays, but its

natural beauty can be lost or enhanced, depending on how it is finished.

New wood can often look unnaturally bright, almost sterile, while the A & B-type wood bleaches tend to leave the wood looking more like a bleached bone found in the desert than warm maple, birch or ash. So I would recommend to any restorer to view as many similar vehicles as they can to try to find

Spending time researching the varieties of wood stain and varnish available will prevent your vehicle ending up like a patchwork quilt.

Applying colour and varnish to wood not only adds an additional preservative layer, it also enhances the wood's natural beauty.

There are some superb products and finishes available to the twenty-first century restorer and vehicle builder, which will give years of enhanced beauty.

the wood effect that they find most pleasing and natural.

Colour and patina can be added to wood in a variety of ways to enhance its overall appearance. For best results you should look to colour the wood before varnishing takes place, as you'll need to keep each process completely separate. Yes, there are tinted varnishes out there, but they are not right for our vehicles, and you could easily turn the wood from light to dark long before you have built up sufficient varnish.

Most wood stains can be wiped on with a rag and will be touch dry within five to ten minutes. Additional coats can be applied to suit your personal taste.

STAINING

My personal choice is to use a liquid stain that can be lightly applied using a cloth or rag. The rag can be made damp with water to dilute the strength of the stain, and the result should be touch dry within ten to fifteen minutes, if not more quickly. This means you can see the overall effect fairly promptly, and decide if more stain needs to be applied either to all the wood or just the parts where there's a slight colour variation.

There is a great variety of type and colour of wood stain, ranging from oak and mahogany to beech and pine. Some colours are exactly as they are

A fine artist's brush, dipped in wood stain, can be used to good effect to add and enhance grain patterns.

described on the tin, while others may leave you wondering if you've opened the wrong tin or gone colour blind. Also, some stains will react differently depending on the type of wood they are applied to, such as maple or ash.

Stain will be difficult to remove if applied incorrectly, and you won't want to have to dismantle the body structure and start the bleaching process again if the applied stain does not produce the expected result. A process I've used to help produce the result I'm looking for is to get a small sheet of plywood, say 24 × 24in, of the same thickness and facing that I propose to use on the vehicle, and then affix 6in lengths of picture-frame wood approximately 6in apart. I then purchase a variety of the small 'tester' pots from the local paint/ hardware store containing all the various shades and wood colours that I'm considering.

I then stain small panels with their appropriate edging (using the picture-frame material) and see how individual stains look when dry and how they complement or contrast with each other. Using this method has enabled me to make an 'educated' purchase of big cans of the chosen colours, and not get any nasty surprises when the stain was applied to the vehicle structure.

Ideally you should achieve a good overall colour match before you start varnishing, but you may find that individual pieces or areas may need selective staining after the varnish is applied. I have also found that by using a combination of artists' brushes and/or cheesecloth the stain can be used to selectively enhance certain grain formations and make them more visually attractive.

Richard McCloskey of Rickmack. com has found that wood patina can be reintroduced by mixing up a light home-made stain of artist's oil paint colours 'raw sienna' and 'burnt sienna', along with some thinner and pure boiled linseed oil. He advises stirring the two paints into a mix of ⅓ mineral spirits, ⅓ pure boiled linseed oil and ⅓ lacquer thinner in a quart (1ltr) container, and continues:

Squeeze a couple of toothpaste globs of the raw sienna into the mix and then a small squeeze of the burnt sienna, just a little now, put on the top and shake it up. Mix it very thoroughly.

You will have to shake it up periodically during use as the colour settles out fairly quickly. Keep another cup of the same thinner mix handy, but without any colour added. Mix some of the coloured mix with some of the clear thinner mix, and apply with a brush to some of your bleached wood; let it sit and soak for a few minutes, then wipe it off with a clean rag.

Try a thin mix first and add more colour to the mix if you need it. Remember: *this is art, not science*! With some practice and experimentation you should be able to match the colour of the bleached old wood with the colour of the new wood. You can do this so well that old and new woods will be indistinguishable one from another!

Nothing can be done about weather-checking cracks or dry rot. These injuries are permanent unless you replace the wood pieces that have this type of damage. Note: always try a test piece of wood first, and let the stain/ toner dry for a couple of days before applying your finish.

Another option for adding tone to your wood is Shellac. This is a natural finishing material that comes in 'blond' and 'amber' tones right off the shelf. It makes a wonderful sealer under varnish and even catalyzed urethane as long as it does not have any wax in it. Read the labels. The amber tone is very warm, but again experiment.

You can thin shellac with denatured alcohol. Do not use it under the polyurethanes. Note that shellac is not

Suzy Carr using a coloured pencil to enhance the grain pattern on a newly constructed tailgate to help it match the patina of the rest of the woodie.

Using a smudging effect can help to enhance the natural grain pattern.

A selection of some of the pens and pencils used by Suzy Carr. An eraser is also useful for blurring the lines when appropriate.

generally available in the UK, other than that found in nail varnish, which hardly seems applicable to adding tone to wood.

If you wish to stain your mahogany panelling, there is a myriad of commercial stains available at your hardware or paint store. I have used many different brands, both water-based and solvent-based, most have worked very well. Pick a stain and try a test where it will not show. You might have to mix two stains together to achieve your desired colour.

Now here's a neat trick highlighted by Rick. He advises that if you only want to darken your mahogany stain slightly, try setting all your panelling out in the sun for an hour. Be sure to expose all pieces evenly, as any shaded area will remain lighter! This process works almost magically in your workshop if you leave the panelling exposed to light or even air for a long time, so keep it wrapped up until you are going to work on it.

I picked up another neat trick for enhancing grain patterns, adding patina and generally helping to match the look of new wood to older, existing wood on a visit to the Signal Hill workshops of Wood N'Carr. Whilst chatting to Doug Carr about construction techniques I spied Suzy Carr apparently drawing some measurements on a station wagon door. However, on closer inspection I discovered

Some woods, such as maple, have weak grain patterns that can be 'developed' using pens and pencils to bring out their natural beauty.

that far from marking out measurements, Suzy was indeed drawing on grain and adding patina to new wood to match that already on the car. She used a number of different coloured soft lead pencils to add marks and grain pattern, some of which were 'smudged' using an eraser to make them blend in.

I've personally employed a slightly similar technique using fine artist's brushes, dipped in wood stain, to enhance grain or add it to a piece of wood that looked somewhat plain. However, it made me feel vindicated to know that professionals use the same techniques.

Every piece of wood is unique, and some of the grain patterns that nature produces could almost be considered works of art, so feel free to experiment with some of these techniques to see if you can enhance the beauty of what nature has created.

EPOXY RESIN

One of the most useful tips that I picked up from the professionals and which helped me with my research was the use of clear epoxy resin. Generally this is applied to the wood after it has been bleached, sanded and stained to the required colour, and thus before the varnish coats are applied.

There are various types of epoxy resin available, some of which can be

ABOVE: *Block sanding the epoxy resin coating with increasingly fine sandpaper produces a finish as smooth as glass, which is the perfect base for the varnish.*

The finish that can be achieved using epoxy and high grade varnish, both flattened between each coat.

sprayed (with the right equipment), whilst others are brushable. There are also two-part resins (resin and hardener), as well as single-part formulations. One of the most popular and widely used is that produced by West System.

I saw resins being actively used at Wood N'Carr in California and at Redding Woodworks in Florida, and the coating provided an amazingly hard and durable surface coating, which could be sanded as smooth as glass. Such a finish provides a fantastic base for the varnish, and could probably substantially reduce the number of varnish coats necessary. I've also been told by one restorer that the flattened resin can be machine polished using an electric polisher and the standard pastes and creams normally used in a vehicle bodyshop for colour sanding and polishing new paintwork to provide a glass-like finish. I've yet to try this for myself, however, so cannot confirm whether it works as well as suggested.

VARNISH

So why use varnish? It is an excellent and ancient – according to Rick Mack, Stradivarius mixed his own! – tough,

Ron Heiden is seen here applying the initial coats of varnish to a tailgate using a foam brush.

Rick Mack advises that a woodie kept in daily use with a varnish finish will need to be sanded and revarnished every year or two in order to stay sharp.

reliable and, most importantly, easy-to-apply wood finish. Varnish flows out smoothly all by itself, and you can brush it, spray it, or rub it on with a rag. It is very adaptable, and beautifully lustrous after six or eight coats. Anyone can use it and apply it at home, although it does take time, especially the thorough sandings between coats.

Before we get into the subject of how, why and where to use varnish, we need to address that thorny question of what other forms of surface protection you can apply successfully to wood. In the fifteen years (at the time of writing) that I've been involved in restoring woodies I've heard people argue the case for all sorts of finished coatings – some weird and some wonderful.

I've also found that many bring product experience from a regular job or work to the restoration process – and some just won't be shifted away from a product that has worked well for them in the past, even if it wasn't an automotive application. For example, there are people of diverse professional occu-pation, such as grand piano restorers and general building contractors, who in the course of their trade may have found a wood treatment that works, say, on a dining-room floor or on showpiece furniture kept in an air-conditioned lounge – but will these products be effective on a vehicle?

Some people like to slap on a couple of coats of satin finish and say 'Job done!', whilst others are convinced that the Danish oil seen being used on a furniture restoration television show will work for them. However, whilst anyone is free to choose whatever they want for their vehicles, if they require a long-lasting and original-looking surface treatment, then it surely has to be varnish.

Health and Safety

There is a legal requirement for all varnish and paint manufacturers to provide health and safety advice for the use of their products, and even though this may be the small print on the side of the tin, it pays to familiarize yourself with its key messages. Some of the warnings found on the side of varnish tins may sound obvious, but I'm willing to bet that somebody out there reading this book will probably admit to themselves that they have taken a risk or two when handling varnish.

For instance, it is not recommended to prepare food or drink near varnish, as the solvent vapour can contaminate them. So don't leave your lunch sandwich sitting on a plate in the garage whilst varnishing. Also, many varnishes are flammable (check the label on the tin), so don't apply it near a naked flame, and don't use tools such as a grinder that may give off sparks near an open varnish tin.

Why Varnish?

Ford, GM, Chrysler and every other coachbuilder, whether large or small, who originally produced wooden-framed station wagons used varnish as their primary finishing material. Even the builders of vans, trucks and buses varnished all the wood that was exposed, and much of the wood that was covered up, too.

If you don't have access to a professional spray booth you can protect your workshop from spray and fumes by building a temporary structure out of plastic sheeting or a pop-up pagoda, as seen here. It will also help to minimize dust intrusion into the spraying area.

Wood preservatives were primitive in the 1920s, 1930s, 1940s and even the 1950s compared with the technological and chemical marvels we enjoy today, so varnish was the protection of choice for most types of wooden bodywork. Good stuff then, good stuff now.

Varnish usually comes in gloss and satin finishes, and most vehicles were finished in gloss, straight from the factory. There are some woodies that still have their original varnish today, and sometimes this varnish appears to be satin, but that is most likely due to the effects of weather, sunshine and age.

The only real drawback to varnish was its lack of durability, especially with the earlier formulas. As all woodie owners will have experienced, varnish deteriorates under sun, rain and abrasion, resulting in cracking, splitting and peeling of the finish, leaving the wood unprotected. Rick Mack advises that a woodie kept in daily use with a varnish finish will need to be sanded and revarnished every year or two in order to stay effective.

This requirement for high levels of maintenance was the main reason for the ultimate demise of the woodie wagon as a production vehicle and their low survival rate today. They were difficult and expensive to produce as well, but it was the buying public's inability and/or unwillingness to keep sanding and varnishing the wood that always held sales down, especially after steel-bodied wagons appeared across the world in the early 1950s.

However, Rick tells us that much has changed since the days when woodies were production cars. For instance, varnish has improved greatly, with formulas that have excellent ultra-violet (UV) protection and are much tougher, which translates into a product with much better durability and longevity – although probably the greatest difference between 'then' and 'now' is the simple fact that today few woodies are used as an all-weather daily driver! But all things considered, modern varnish makes an excellent choice for your pampered woodie.

What Varnish to Choose

There will be numerous brand names and a variety of manufacturers to choose from wherever you live, so it pays to do your research, talk to other restorers and ask them what varnishes they use, and then try it out it on a small area. On one of my first visits to a woodie wagon gathering in northern California ('Woodies on the Wharf') I asked several owners of beautifully restored cars how they achieved such a lustrous finish, and they all advised using a yacht varnish. Nevertheless there are many fine brands of varnish on the shelf; Rick advises us as follows:

I like Z-Spar Flagship and epiphanes for their great UV protection, and Z-Spar Captains and Interlux Schooner for their wonderful warm, golden tone – and these also have good UV protection.

Always read the instructions of the brand you choose. Also make sure that you have the correct thinners to match the varnish. It is best to buy varnish by the quart. The gallon is less expensive overall but it will 'skim over' and become useless long before you get to the bottom of the can!

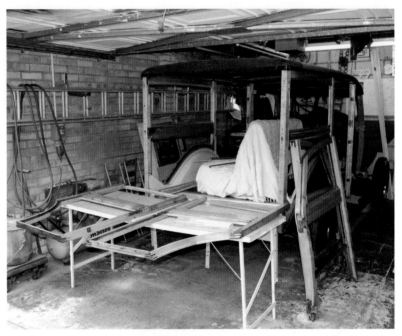

It is up to you where and how you apply the varnish, but this writer has achieved his best results by laying individual items flat on a trestle table.

I also prefer to flat spray varnish on to each and every component as an individual item. Others may prefer to spray the finished door, say, as one complete part – but that's just personal taste.

If you choose to spray varnish the entire body, make sure you mask off anything you don't want varnished, such as tyres, paintwork, glass and engine.

Some woodies have painted metal panels instead of plywood inserts, so if you are painting them it is essential to mask the woodwork very well: removing overspray from your freshly varnished woodwork will be a headache you can easily avoid.

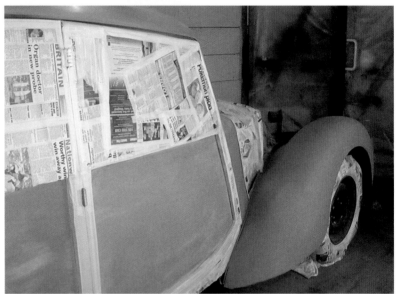

Even when carrying out only a small paintwork repair it is advisable to mask the entire bodywork to avoid damaging the varnish.

URETHANES

Urethanes are automotive clear coats, and they are really tough! They require a catalyst, they must be sprayed, and they can be toxic. You will need a ventilated spray booth and a quality respirator, and an inexpensive spray suit would be advisable as well. If you can put this package in place, you can quickly shoot a super-durable finish on to your wood, which will last a lifetime. You can also spray three coats at a time, claims Rick Mack.

Urethane glosses out like polished glass and cures out in a few days as hard as nails – and it is flexible, too. All automotive paint companies produce a catalysed urethane for clear coats. Rick tells us that he has been using Du Pont V-7600S with terrific results, and claims that no tougher or glossier finish is available! Rick advises:

> I do love varnish, but the catalyzed urethanes get my vote for the best finish that you can buy! But a word of caution: because of the high VOC and toxic nature of this material, it is not for everyone, and it is not readily available in California – at least it isn't supposed to be. So check with your local auto paint store or local body shop.
>
> This is real high-tech stuff and you must follow the manufacturer's instructions precisely! Urethanes are not zen.
>
> There are other choices, too. I understand that some similar finishing materials are now available which are 'water-based', although I have no experience to date with any of these products. Eventually all finishes will have to be water-based and environmentally friendly, and this is a very good idea, especially if these products can be made to be as tough as the solvent-based finishes I am familiar with. Time will tell.

POLYURETHANES

There is another class of finishes known as polyurethanes, which are readily available at all hardware stores. They can be applied with a brush or sprayed on, in a way very similar to varnish products, but they are different chemically from the varnishes. Some are

James at Woodies is seen here demonstrating the delicate art of scraping off small spots of varnish from the rear fender. Trying to sand out the marks could result in having to sand and polish the whole panel.

water-based, too. They are very durable and easy to apply, but their down side is that they do not have any tone.

Polyurethanes are clear, though some have a slightly cold or blue cast to them, which is unsightly on wood. Rick adds: 'I much prefer the appearance of varnish, but if you are looking for a super clear finish that can be applied with a brush at home, polyurethane may be for you. If you are going to use polyurethanes, you can follow the same instructions as for sanding and applying varnish.'

WOOD PREPARATION: SANDING

It is very important to sand the wood smooth before applying any varnish. No matter which finish you choose for your woodie, you will need to sand the wood thoroughly before applying it. This process is always the same, today as yesterday, and there are no short cuts.

For new wood, or old wood in good condition, use a random orbital sander (at the time of writing Dewalt makes the best). Start with 80 grit to get out any heavy scratches or divots and to

get off the dark, weathered top layer of the wood. Wear a dust mask!

After the 80 grit, move on to sanding all the wood again with 100 grit, which gets rid of the scratches left by the 80 grit, then sand all again with 150 grit to remove the scratches left by the 100 grit. In most cases, sanding down to 150 grit is more than adequate, though you could maybe sand down to 180 grit if you are obsessive. Further sanding with finer sandpaper on hardwood becomes an exercise in futility and can actually smooth the wood so much that it has no 'tooth' to hold the finish! It is advisable to dust off the wood between sanding grits so that no errant pieces of sand from the previous grit remain, as these will put those nasty little circular scratches into your wood.

You must be sure to look very carefully for any remaining heavy scratches – they will appear under good light after you have finished sanding with 150 grit. If you do not find them and sand them out now, they will surely be visible after you have applied the finish, so take your time here.

If you need to bleach your old wood, do your full regime of sanding first!

After bleaching, you can only sand with 180 grit or 220 grit by hand to smooth out the fuzz raised by the bleaching process. The bleached layer of the wood is not very deep and it sands off easily.

When sanding softwoods such as mahogany, you will certainly need to sand down to 180 grit, and perhaps down to 220 grit. If you plan to stain your mahogany panels the extra fine sanding will assure that there will be no tiny swirl marks left to trap the stain and look ugly under the varnish. But remember: panelling veneer is very thin, so be careful not to sand through it!

After sanding thoroughly working through the grits with the random orbital sander, you might consider taking some 180 grit or 220 grit sandpaper in your hand and smoothing out the edges and corners of the hardwood and the difficult-to-reach inside corners. Note that varnish or any other finish will not stick well to a blade edge, so always ease the edges at least a little. As you probably know, it is best to sand 'with the grain'.

Your new wood and old wood should now be ready for application of the finish.

APPLYING VARNISH

When applying varnish, start with a 1½in brush. It can be an inexpensive one since we are first going to apply varnish coats to obtain a 'build', meaning some thickness of coats on the wood before we worry about sanding it smooth. You can use a throw-away 'sponge' brush on the flat panelling, but sponges do not work well on the structural wood parts with edges, curves, reliefs and corners.

Pour some varnish from your can into a separate cup, having estimated how much you are actually going to use. Never varnish directly from the can as doing so will quickly contaminate your remaining varnish with 'crud' known as 'inclusion bodies', which will lump up your subsequent coats. If you have varnish left over in the cup when you are done finishing for the day, paint it on the dog house or maybe on the hidden areas of your wood or on the backside of your panelling – but don't pour it back into the can!

Before you start varnishing, it is a very good idea to clean off all the wood that you have carefully laid out to varnish. Try using a soft dust brush first, then a vacuum cleaner or air blower (blowing the wood dust around can be a problem), then wipe with a cotton rag dampened with paint thinner and allow to dry. Finally, go over the wood completely with a tack cloth. The cleaner you can get the wood, the better the varnish finish will be!

The First Varnish Coat

There are at least two different theories about the first varnish coat: I feel that the first coat should be thinned as much as 50 per cent with the appropriate thinner for the varnish that you have chosen. Read the labels on the can regarding thinners: the theory is that the first coat will soak deep into the wood. Be especially thorough about wetting the open end grain to seal it against moisture; some woodie manufacturers actually soaked the wood in varnish to seal it!

Another theory is to use the varnish straight from the can without thinning. Perhaps reading the instructions on the can is the best way to go about this: most brands recommend thinning by about 20 per cent on the first coat.

With my 1½in brush, I apply a 50/50 thinned mix of varnish, working quickly to get the wood thoroughly coated. Work a single piece of wood, or a single unit such as a door, at one time so you can be thorough and maintain control. After you become adept at varnishing you can work larger areas or multiple units. You may brush cross-grain or any way you choose to get the varnish on to the wood, then once it is completely wet, change to quickly brushing out the varnish with the grain so it flows out smoothly. Thoroughly saturate the end grains with this thin coat.

If you are working on an assembled unit such as a door, pick a piece of wood at the top, varnish it completely, stroke it out with the grain, then move on to the next attached piece of wood and follow the same procedure. Try to keep a 'wet edge' when varnishing, not letting the varnish dry before continuing on from the last point with new varnish.

This takes a little practice, as you must move down a door in several directions at the same time. This is why you will need to work quickly. However, varnish is really forgiving and multiple coats will cover any missed spots – though try not to leave too many missed spots during each coat. After a couple of coats you will gain more control and find your own rhythm and style of applying varnish.

Subsequent Coats

After you have varnished your wood pieces with the 50/50 thinned mix, let the varnish dry for eight or ten hours, then go right back and apply a second coat of the same thinned mix. As long as you do not wait any longer in between the first and second coat, the second coat will stick just fine. If you wait a day, you will need to sand lightly with 220 grit or a scotch pad so the next coat will stick.

Let the second coat dry completely, perhaps taking two days. Now sand lightly with 220 grit and follow up with a scotch pad to completely dull the surface for the next coat to stick. These two thinned coats of varnish are not yet thick enough to sand aggressively.

Clean the sanded surface with a thinner rag, then a tack cloth, and mix up a third coat of varnish. This time you need to mix 25 per cent thinner with 75 per cent varnish. Do read the instructions on the can regarding just what to use as a proper thinner for your selected varnish. Apply a third coat of the 75/25 varnish/thinner mix and allow it to dry completely. Then scuff it thoroughly with a scotch pad, clean the wood and apply a fourth coat of the 75/25 mix. Let it dry completely. Scuff this fourth coat thoroughly with the scotch pad.

For the fifth and subsequent coats, you want to thin the varnish 10 to 20 per cent, depending on the ambient temperature. You can use varnish at full strength here, but it will not flow well if the weather is too warm. When your brush 'drags', you need to thin the varnish. Varnishing is a matter of 'feel' and varies from person to person.

After you have five or six coats of varnish on your wood, you can begin to sand more aggressively with 320 or 400 grit sandpaper between coats. Be careful of sanding too much on the edges, however, as it is easy to sand through to bare wood. In fact it is a good idea to avoid sanding the edges with sandpaper, and to just touch them lightly with a scotch pad to give them a 'tooth'.

The more coats you have, the cleaner you need to get your wood before applying the next coat of varnish. When you have successfully applied seven or eight coats, you are ready to apply a 'last' coat.

Wipe that wood really clean and apply a last coat thinned at about 15 per cent. When it is dry, check it out: how does it look? Did you get a lot of junk in it? You can sand out a few lumps with 600–1,000 grit wet and dry sandpaper, then rub it out with polish, but if this coat has too many 'inclusion bodies' you will need to sand and apply another 'final' coat. Use your best brush on these last coats and clean them after use with plenty of mineral spirits/paint thinner, but not lacquer thinner.

Much of this varnish work is a learning experience and needs some getting used to before you will find your own rhythm and style. Deciding when the job is done is a kind of judgement call as well. Basically you are done when you are satisfied that the varnish looks good and feels good to you.

There are other approaches to thinning, to sanding and to varnishing. I have one friend who always uses varnish straight from the can without thinning at all! He puts it into a separate cup before applying it. He also sands solely with 150 grit in between coats, a grit which seems a little too rough for me, but his varnish work is always superb!

Another friend, who restores wooden boats, only uses Epiphanes varnish and thins the first few coats 50/50, then applies some at 60/40, then some at 75/25 until he reaches sixteen or eighteen coats – all with a sponge brush! But his boats are spectacular! These differences in procedures and approaches are really a tribute to just how versatile and forgiving varnish is! You will have to find a varnish regime that works for you.

The final varnish coats can be sprayed, of course – for that matter, all the varnish coats can be sprayed, although I feel that the first coats are easier to control with a brush during application. The brush also allows you to fully saturate and better seal the end grains of the wood.

APPLYING URETHANES

Urethane finishes can be applied directly to the wood, but I recommend using some kind of sealer first, especially on the soft mahogany panels. Many sealers are available commercially: water-white lacquer, acrylic, epoxy and shellac, to name but a few. I have used all these types with excellent results, but prefer to use Smith's epoxy, which is a two-part, A & B chemistry, mixed 1:1 for application. It is very thin and soaks deep into the wood, and seals it against water quite well. All types of finish can be applied over it.

Testing Sealers and Finishes for Use on Stained Panelling

If you choose to use a sealer, apply it according to the manufacturer's instructions, then let it dry and sand it smooth with 220 grit to 400 grit sandpaper; clean the wood so that it is as dust free as possible, as you would before applying varnish. After dusting it off, the wood should be moved into a suitable spray booth and tacked off again.

Following the manufacturer's instructions exactly, mix the urethane that you have chosen. Mix only as much as you think you will need, perhaps a pint or a quart. This material is expensive! Note that urethane is absolutely clear and has no tone, so if you wish the wood to appear warm and golden as it does with a varnish finish, you will need to tone the urethane with DMX dyes: these are available through your local auto paint stores, where they are known as 'radiance' colours. You only need a small amount of DMX #212 red and DMX yellow (they only make one yellow). Take your own little bottles, with good, tight tops, to the paint store; you will need no more than an ounce of each colour. The DMX red is more intense than the DMX yellow.

Try a mix of one drop of red and four drops of yellow to each pint of your clear urethane. Use a small dropper, not a big one: drops can vary greatly in size, so try to standardize the drop size; add more colour if you need it. Do a test first on some scrap wood. Test, test and test again.

Put on your respirator, go into the booth, load your spray gun with your mixed urethane and spray on three coats, waiting about fifteen minutes in between coats for the clear to 'flash'. Let the finish dry for at least a day, maybe two, then wet sand with 400 grit to 600 grit using a rubber pad under the sandpaper 'block sanding'.

Watch those edges: don't sand through the finish on them! Clean and tack the wood, and spray three more coats in the same manner as the first three. The soft mahogany might need an extra shoot of two or three coats as it is very absorbent.

Let the clear dry for a couple of days. You might have to sand out a few 'inclusion bodies' with 1,000 grit or 1,500 grit and then polish out the wood with fine polishing compound. This final step takes some time, but can make for a super smooth and glossy finish – just like a custom paint job! Varnish can be polished out in the same fashion, but it takes longer to cure before it can be successfully polished or hand-rubbed out.

If you are unfamiliar with spraying automotive paints, you should seek some professional help or choose to use brushed-on varnish as a finish. The urethane finish is super tough and glossy but it is high tech and requires some advanced knowledge to use properly.

One of the above methods of finishing should work for you – though it's not a bad idea to find some wood to practise on before you start on your woodie. Good luck and good finishing!

IN CONCLUSION

Most of the words of wisdom in this chapter have been very kindly supplied by Rick Mack, who specializes in 1949–51 Ford woodies at his Tacoma, Washington, workshops, and I am indebted to him for both the volume and quality of the material he has supplied. The information is so comprehensive, covering all aspects and methods of applying a finish to your wooden vehicle, that there's very little to add.

Obviously the measurements and products that Rick mentions may not be available in your part of the world, but converting quarts to litres and ounces to grams is quite straightforward.

CHAPTER 16

Woodgraining

Woodgraining is the practice of applying a woodgrain effect to a non-wood surface and thus creating the illusion of a wood finish. It also helps to increase the natural beauty and appeal of that surface.

The process of applying a woodgrain finish to vehicle dashboards and door and window mouldings was used extensively by automakers and coachbuilders from the 1920s to the mid-1950s, but today it's an art form that can be re-created with a little patience, skill and the right tools. Grain-It Technologies of Winter Haven, Florida, is one of the world's foremost exponents of automotive woodgraining techniques, and so I asked company founder, Evan Westlake, to tell us something about the history of woodgraining. He tells us:

Woodgraining, sometimes referred to as 'faux finishing', has been around for thousands of years, but witnessed a big resurgence in popularity during the neo-classical revival period of the nineteenth century when artists would apprentice for ten years or more with a master woodgrainer before they could work on their own. Great recognition was awarded to artists who could trick people into thinking that their work was the real thing.

Whilst early forms of woodgraining were achieved by a lithographed process, the contoured printing method was developed in Europe, and in 1918 this process was used for the first time in the US on the stamped steel cases produced by the National Cash Register (NCR) company – in fact over one million were produced using this method.

Woodgraining witnessed another revival during the Art Deco period of the 1920s and 1930s, and this resulted in Ford introducing the process in 1930 on its Model A. As a result, Ford became the first of more than sixty-five American automakers to use the woodgraining process in the years to follow.

In 1931 NCR sold its woodgraining technology and patents to the Oxford Ink & Varnish Corporation of Detroit, Michigan, and as a result they designed and manufactured the plates and rollers used in the woodgraining process and then leased them to the US automakers. Under this scheme Oxford received a royalty of one cent for each square foot of surface finished on the amount of product produced. Oxford also supplied the automakers with all the primers, inks, pastes and finishing materials, and as a result the contoured printing process was used in the US auto industry until the mid-1950s.

Applying a woodgrain effect to a non-wood surface, such as a dashboard, can turn function into beauty.

Cadillac was one of more than sixty-five US automakers to apply woodgraining to their dashboards during the 1930s.

Today, Grain-It uses the original woodgraining process used by Oxford and has over a hundred original preserved Oxford woodgrain artworks.

THE DI-NOC PROCESS

No chapter on woodgraining would be complete without reference to the Di-Noc process. As there seems to be some confusion between the original Di-Noc process and the material available today, I asked Evan Westlake to put the record straight. He explains:

The woodgrain pattern on this 1936 Ford 'Phaeton' convertible was subtle yet refined.

In 1926 GM acquired auto hardware producer, Ternstedt, as part of its purchase of Fishers Bodies Company. In 1930 Ternstedt became a division of GM, and in 1936 the company began to produce photo plates based on Oxford's designs and patents. A patent infringement lawsuit followed, which resulted in both companies going back to the drawing board, so to speak. However, it also led indirectly to the development of the Di-Noc process by GM.

There are many misconceptions about Di-Noc, but hopefully a quote from the 1939–40 Fishers body service manual should clarify things. This states: 'Di-Noc Production Transfer: This production transfer is used in body production and is applied on sheets of metal after the ground colour is applied to the sheet. It is simply a designed graining that is transferred from its paper foundation on to the fresh, tacky, coloured lacquer that has been previously prepared. The sheet metal, after the transfer has been applied, *is then stamped or pressed* between dies to form an instrument panel, globe box lid, garnish moulding or any other formed panel. This type of transfer is not to be used for service repair.'

The key message here is that the Di-Noc process was applied before the metal was stamped out. This process worked because the nitro-cellulose film being applied to the fresh tacky lacquer base became part of the finish. This meant that the 'film' could never be lifted or separated from the metalwork.

Today's Di-Noc, on the other hand, is more of a vinyl decal film as you obviously can't have your old dashboard restamped with the original Di-Noc process.

The first part of the process is to strip the dashboard to bare metal and fill any imperfections with a light coating of filler.

Use an acid-etch primer on the bare metal to give future coatings a good key …

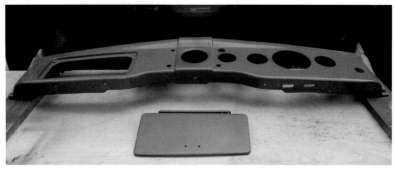

… then apply a high build primer to cover any small scratch marks.

REPLICATION NOT RESTORATION

So, whilst there is no engineering process that can today mechanically replicate the original Di-Noc application, which used Oxford plates as part of transfer application process, you can achieve exactly the same original look and finish today by using the contoured printing method. Copies of the original artwork used by Oxford are now used by Grain-It in their contoured printing method so you can match the original pattern exactly. Grain-It can also photograph and scan any original piece of woodgrain and then make a plate from which you can achieve an exact copy of the original.

Whilst many aspects of auto restoration focus on the repairing and rebuilding of the original parts or components, a woodgrained finish on a metal dashboard, garnish moulding or window frame is not something that can be repaired in the normal sense of the word. It can, however, be re-created using various techniques.

As will have been repeated many times and in many previous chapters of this book, different techniques, processes and even materials were used in different parts of the world, and the same is true today when looking at the replication process. So as I have enlisted the help of a range of specialists in different fields of expertise and in different towns, cities and countries, so we'll explore the solutions they suggest on a regional basis, where appropriate.

Recreating the Original Look

US-based Grain-It is the obvious choice for any American restorer, and it's a system that should work anywhere in the world to give outstanding results, providing all the relevant inks, paints, solutions and liquids can be acquired. However, it's worth bearing in mind that the international transportation of solvents and flammable liquids, such as paints, means that the company's range of paints, solvents and lacquers cannot be shipped internationally unless you are prepared to use purpose-made sealed containers that would cost many hundreds of any currency unit to ship.

However, there are some locally sourced products that work well with the Grain-It system, and these will be covered later in this chapter.

PUTTING A BASE ON BARE METAL

Unless you are 100 per cent confident of your skills and the materials you are handling, I would strongly recommend using another car part or scrap piece of metal as a sample tester. This can be used to trial all the materials used in the woodgraining process and to experiment with the various tools; you can double check drying times and ensure you don't get any unwanted surface reactions. So, let's assume that you'll be treating the 'sample' to all the processes described below.

Whilst the finishing processes for both aluminium and steel are exactly the same, preparing the base metal requires different techniques. Aluminium, by its very nature, is much softer than steel, so removing any existing surface coating should be done carefully so as not to scuff or scratch the surface. A chemical paint stripper and/or light surface sanding should be all that is needed to produce a clean, bare surface. Avoid using any powered sanders or grit-blasting cabinets or you'll create yourself a lot of work getting the surface really smooth again. Grain-It recommends using an acid-etch primer on aluminium to help bond with the surface.

Unlike aluminium, steel dashboards or panels can rust quite badly, and so bead blasting might be the best solu-tion to removing a heavy surface corrosion. A high-build primer can then be used on both aluminium and steel dashboards and will help to cover small imperfections, scratches and pitting. A red oxide primer would be perfect. Any imperfections in the metal's surface are best dealt with at this stage, so it should be sanded and re-coated as many times as is needed to obtain a smooth and scratch-free finish.

The next stage is to apply the base coat, which needs to be matched as near as possible to the original factory base coat in order to provide the correct contrast and colour. Even a heavily rusted or sun-bleached dashboard will usually have some of the original base coat hidden away in a corner, edge, behind a switch or ash tray or, more often, on the reverse side.

Restorers in the USA can take advantage of the wide range of original base colours offered by Grain-It, and its DVDs provide a step-by-step guide to applying the paint and will recommend how many spray cans will be needed. When going down this route it is as well to be a little generous on the amount of paint you might need, as it is better to have one can too many than too little paint and run the risk of having to re-order and then getting a can from a batch of a different mix.

Evan Westlake, one of the founders of Grain-It, is emphatic that whilst you can order your base coat from a local paint store or supplier, which you can use with your own spray equipment, you must use DuPont Chromabase®. He tells us: 'This paint dries to a flat finish and the ink used in our process dries right into the paint. If you try to use a regular gloss automotive paint as a base the ink may never be absorbed or dry properly and the results will be disastrous.'

I mentioned previously the importance of dealing with any imperfections in the metal's surface at the primer stage, and this cannot be overstressed. The technical manual for DuPont Chromabase® advises that it is not for sale to the general public, and because it contains isocyanates it should not be sanded, once applied, without a NIOSH-approved air-purifying respirator with particulate filters or appropriate ventilation, and gloves.

TYPES OF WOODGRAIN EFFECT

Grain-It has acquired the artwork of a large number of Oxford original patterns and designs, and from these has produced eighteen printing plates that cover virtually every single woodgrain application used on American cars. Two plate sizes are available, depending on your individual requirements. Interestingly, Evan Westlake points out: 'Straight grain was the most commonly used. Even if the dashboard was done in burl walnut, the window frames would have been done in a straight grain.'

Here, in brief, are the grain patterns currently available from Grain-It:

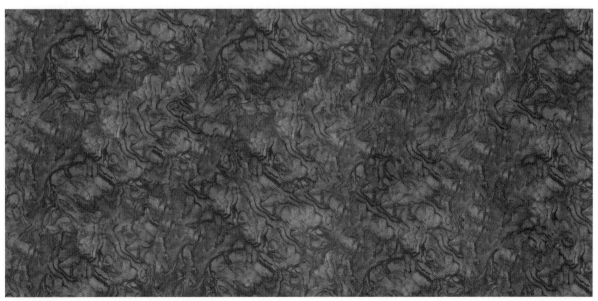

Burl walnut is one of the most popular woodgraining effects.

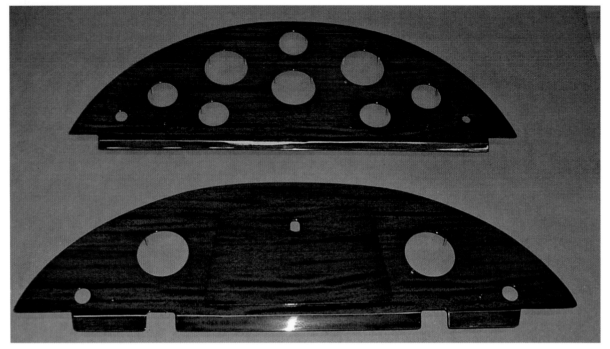

Mahogany graining can be used to fantastic effect.

Straight grain: Can be used to create a walnut, maple or mahogany effect – it just depends on the choice of base colour and the graining compound.

Butt walnut: A highly figured pattern with a mirror image in the centre that flows out on both sides. One advantage of having a larger plate with this pattern is that you get the full mirror image – you only get a proportion of the image with the smaller plate.

Burl walnut: Once again the bigger sheet gives the full mirror image.

Mahogany: Used extensively in the 1920s – the plate creates a ribbon mahogany pattern.

Primavera mahogany: A straight grain with vertical figuring; it is used on some Buicks and Cadillacs.

Stipple mahogany: A very fine grain used, for instance, on the Ford Model A.

Crotch mahogany: Used mostly in the early 1930s. It is taken from the centre of the tree and gives a mirrored image.

African stump mahogany: Used mostly in the late 1920s and early 1930s.

Sapele: Used on 1946–48 Ford and Mercury wagons and convertibles.

Curly maple: Used on the garnish mouldings on the 1940 Ford.

Bird's eye maple: Used extensively on the exterior of cars such as the Chevy, Pontiac and Buick 'tin' woodies.

Heavy bird's eye maple: A pretty pattern, but not used all that extensively by US automakers.

Quilted maple: Could be used on exteriors, such as on 'tin' woodies.

Oriental wood: A wider straight grain with more solid lines, used by late model Packards, such as the 1946–48 and also on the 1949 Plymouth.

Zebrano: A wide-striped grain with speckled figuring between the grains; actually used on some aircraft panels.

Redwood burl: A tighter grain pattern.

Mottled aspen: Used almost exclusively on late 1930s Packards.

Oak: A very pretty straight grain pattern, but not used very much. Many people used this pattern on doors and interior finishes.

PREPARING TO WOODGRAIN

Care of the Printing Plates

A word of warning: the plates do not have a protective coating on them, although it may look like it, so do not try to peel off any edges of coatings otherwise you'll ruin the plate and make it unusable. Some plates have a purple finish and some don't, but either finish works exactly the same.

Before using a Grain-It printing plate for the very first time it is recommended that you rinse it off with water and then dry it with a paper towel. It's then ready to use – it's as simple as that. After use you should use a wax or grease remover to clean the plate.

Care of the Roller

The sponge roller head in the Grain-It kit comes packed with a light dusting of powder to help keep the roller dry in transit: this needs to be washed in soap water and gently massaged by hand to ensure all powder particles are washed off. Rinse it off and then let it air dry, or use a lint-free towel.

Once in use the roller head will get stained, but they seem to work better that way.

Prepping the Dashboard

The application of surface primers and base coats has been covered in a previous section, but before you start rollering on the grain pattern it's worth thinking about ensuring that you have good access to the parts to be woodgrained, and that they are not likely to move when the roller is applied.

In some cases you might need to turn or rotate the part as the roller is applied, so think about either mounting the parts in a way that you can get clear access on all sides, or perhaps persuade a friend to hold the parts.

Woodgraining Inks

Woodgraining inks are available in a variety of colours, which makes the combination of grain pattern and overall visual effect almost endless. Grain-It supplies its inks in plastic tubs, and once opened for use you will need to remove the skin that forms on the top of the ink before use. Stir up the contents a little and then apply some to the printing plate, spreading it out with the doctor blade. Go one way and then back again, keeping the bevelled edge towards the direction of travel.

Put the roller at one edge of the woodgraining plate and roll it towards the other edge of the plate. The roller will pick up the etched woodgrain pattern so that it can now be printed on to the part – but do not let the woodgrain pattern overlap on the roller!

APPLYING THE GRAIN

Place the roller on the part and roll out the pattern, making sure you stop before you reach the end of the impregnated pattern. Depending on the circumference of the roller you may, for instance, roll out 12 inches of pattern in one go, but do make sure you stop before you reach the end of the pattern. You will only pick up inked pattern on the roller for one revolution, and if you attempt to go beyond this the results will be poor.

After every single application clean the roller by rolling it back and forth on craft paper. This will remove any leftover graining compound. Now set the roller aside whilst you prepare for the next application.

Place blending paper, rough side down, on top of the wet pattern you've just printed, carefully lining up the edge of the paper with the edge of the printed pattern. Hold the paper in place with magnets (this will not damage the fresh print) and wipe clean the area around the joint so that the new application does not overlap any old ink.

Squeegee the printing plate again, pick up the pattern on the roller and lay the inked roller on top of the blending paper and roll it forwards. Take the magnets off, and lift the blending paper off the part. This process should

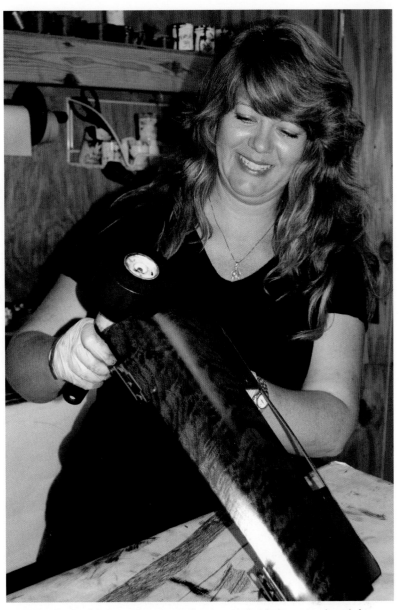

Grain-It's LeAnn Westlake is seen demonstrating how to apply the inked pattern to the end of a dashboard section.

Some components will require two or more passes (even using the largest roller) to print the full woodgrain pattern. Here we can clearly see where the pattern ends on the roller, and it is essential not to try to print beyond that point.

LeAnn is seen here using a small brush to lightly blend in the areas where two roller applications meet, thus making for an invisible join.

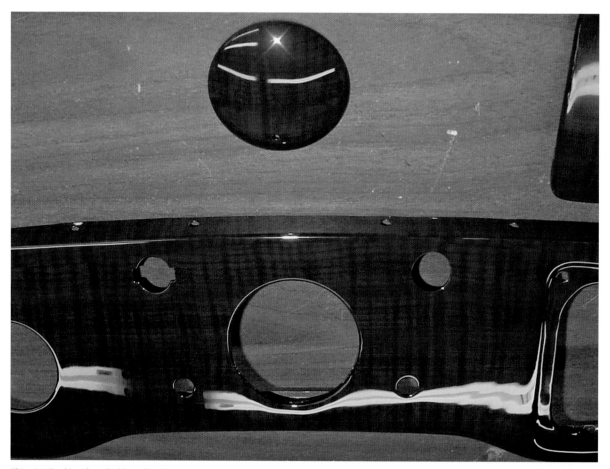

This 1936 Ford Roadster dashboard highlights the unique effects that can be recreated. This example was woodgrained using the curly maple plate but with mahogany base colour, graining and toning compounds. Only the Roadster received this particular woodgraining effect in 1936.

When properly applied, woodgraining can look every bit as good, if not better than real wood.

produce an almost invisible line, but an eraser pencil or fine paintbrush may be needed to blend the two applications.

Squeegee the woodgraining plate again, and repeat the process until the part is completely printed. Clean the roller and set it aside. Please note that you must squeegee the plate between each application, and you must clean the roller on clean paper between each roll.

Drying Time

It is essential to let the graining compound dry completely on all parts before doing anything else. Depending on the temperature and the humidity, the drying time could vary from a few days to a few weeks, so please be prepared to be patient. However, the Grain-It team have recently introduced a 'lock-down coat', which will help

speed up drying time to within twenty-four hours. However, it is advisable to wait at least twenty-four hours after printing and before misting the lockdown coat. Test with a finger to ensure the ink is dry – if it is still tacky, let it dry for longer.

It is almost impossible to mail, courier or ship solvents internationally these days, but if you live in a region where Grain-It can ship the 'lock-down coat'

Woodgraining has been used here to good effect on the dashboard and steering column of this Ford woodie being constructed at Treehouse Woodies, to help blend the metalwork in with the real wood.

This stunning dashboard was woodgrained in the traditional way by James McIntytre at Mac's Pinstriping in Houston, Texas. James prefers to use artist's acrylic paints, such as those available from Proceed, and judging by the results achieved it shows what you can do with a few old brushes and rags, and lots of artistic talent.

Here's a nice example of a GM 'Faux' woodie sporting everything but the kitchen sink.

Woodgraining was used to good effect on early 1950 steel-bodied GM station wagons.

then do use it, applying a light misting coat. In other parts of the world you will just have to exercise restraint and wait until the compound dries naturally.

Toner Application

Once you have finished all the woodgraining and allowed it to dry thoroughly, you may then apply the toner. This will make the woodgrain look richer and will help hide any blending. To apply the toner, take your pallet knife and remove the surface skin and then stir thoroughly.

Next apply a small amount of toner to a soft paper towel and gently wipe it on to the surface, much as you would apply a wax or a polish, covering the entire surface area. Work it into crevices and blend everything together to give

it that richness and beauty associated with natural wood. Finally, using light hand movements, immediately wipe off any surplus toner with a clean paper towel, to leave a very thin transparent coat of tone on the printed surface.

Once you are satisfied with the result, allow it to dry. A light dusting with the lock-down coat will help to advance the curing process (it can be applied approximately thirty minutes after the toner has been applied), speeding up the final drying time to within twenty-four hours.

The Finishing Coat

The finishing coat is one of the stages where the value of the 'sample' piece you have produced in tandem with the genuine vehicle parts will come into

its own. There are a great many brands, types and finishes when it comes to clearcoats, and I have had mixed results with them all – some have crazed whilst others have dulled when dry. Temperature and humidity can affect the resulting finish tremendously, and I would recommend using either a lacquer or high build urethane high gloss finish. Either way, try it on your sample piece first, and start with a dusting coat before trying to float a river of clearcoat across the surface, as this will almost certainly craze and crack when it dries.

PAINTED-ON WOODGRAIN

Before we finish this section on woodgraining it's worth taking a quick look at the age-old art of woodgraining as a painted-on finish. This type of woodgraining is often referred to as scumbling, which is the process of laying one colour over another to create a broken colour effect. In the 1920s, 1930s, 1940s and even the 1950s this type of painted-on woodgrain proved particularly popular when large areas had to be covered to give an upmarket effect. Typical applications were wood-panelled doors, and bus and railway carriage interiors.

Whilst it may not have been used originally on car dashboards and mouldings, it has certainly proved popular in recent years amongst vehicle enthusiasts and restorers who wish to re-create a woodgrain effect. On the positive side, the tools needed to start the process are cheap and easy to acquire, often constituting little more than some old shaped paintbrushes, rubber combs and a coarse-grain rag.

On the negative side the process requires a lot of skill on the part of the person applying the graining, and most of the people who achieve good results have either studied the subject at college or been doing it for a very long time. Real wood has so many intricate patterns within the grain, and trying to replicate this at the first, or even the tenth attempt, is not for everybody. It's almost on a par with trying to teach somebody to paint an award-winning landscape with some artist materials they picked up at a flea market – it could fill a whole book on the subject!

So for this very reason I will not be going into this subject in great detail in this chapter. It's a niche art form that may be taught at a college near you – but then again it may not. Here in the UK we have the Association of Painting Craft Teachers (www.apct.co.uk), which runs occasional woodgraining courses, and they have produced some training DVDs covering oak, burr walnut and mahogany graining techniques; these are available from A. S. Handover Ltd, London (www.handover.co.uk).

WATER TRANSFER PRINTING

As if to prove that processes are constantly changing as a result of technological advances, a new state-of-the-art woodgraining technique is evolving in a process currently known as water transfer printing. Also known as hydrographics, immersion printing or even 'dipping', the process was originally developed in Japan and patented as cubic printing.

In simple terms, the process involves the application of a pre-printed PVA-based film, or decal, to the surface of a component via a water bath. This simple yet effective process can apply thousands of designs covering a virtually endless range of subjects such as natural materials – animal fur, lizard skins, flowers and stone patterns – through to designs more suited to automotive applications such as carbon fibre, camouflage and, of course, hundreds of woodgrains and patterns.

Woodgraining can turn a faux woodie into a real head-turner!

After stripping off the old varnish and paint the dashboard needs to be re-finished in the correct base coat to contrast with the coloured film. Depending on the chosen wood effect this may require a pinkish or orange base.

To make things even more complicated the vast range of wood designs is also available in a variety of colours and intensity. In essence, you are spoilt for choice.

Firms offering a water transfer printing process generally prefer to tackle the whole job themselves, which includes stripping (bead blasting if required), priming and prepping the dashboard, facia panels and door trims. Some firms will accept parts that you've prepared yourself, but usually offer no guarantee as to the quality of the end result.

Anybody who has done any form of woodgraining will understand that the finished result is usually based on a combination of at least two colours – for instance, a light base coat followed by a darker grain pattern and possibly finished off with some sort of toning compound. Certain wood effects may require a pinkish or orange base coat, and if you get this wrong the overall effect might not be too pleasing. It is for this reason that coating firms prefer to handle the entire process so that the end result will be perfect.

However, for the purpose of this book I found a firm here in the UK that

was not only happy for me to do all the 'prep' work myself, but also gave me helpful advice on base coat colour. Wicked Coatings of Poole in Dorset is run by Lyle Meikle and Chris Hinks and started life as a regular auto-body repair business. These two first heard about hydrographics in 2010, decided to test the market, and now employ eight people in a specialized coatings business.

Once the dashboard has been removed from the vehicle it needs to be prepared for the new surface coating. I opted to use chemical stripper to remove all traces of paint, and then to sand it smooth and apply coats of two-part etch primer: primer filler (to help cover any fine scratches or blemishes) and then a coloured top coat, as recommended by Wicked Coatings. Metal dashboards were usually stamped out with little thought that anybody might ever be sanding them again, and I found to my cost that an MGB dashboard had some fairly sharp edges, one of which sliced the top of my finger so I had to take a two-week break from wet-sanding and spray paint … so please take care.

Obviously paint processes and possibly the chemical make-up of the films (many of which are produced in China) vary, so you'll need to check locally with your chosen coatings firm, but Lyle and Chris at Wicked Coatings recommended the paint I should use. They said that this offered the best adhesion with the PSA film, and this has certainly proved correct.

Having previously chosen a burl walnut pattern for the dashboard on my 1936 Ford V8 woodie, on arrival at the Poole workshops I was offered a choice of colour intensities. Holding the film across the dash gave me a chance to see how the various colour options would look, and so I made my choice. In no time at all the film was cut to length and being gently floated on to the surface of the warm water tank. Once activated by a chemical spray the dashboard parts were ready to be gently rolled into the floating film.

The result is both instantly and truly amazing. There is no slow build-up as with other process – water transfer printing is instant. Once out of the tank the parts are thoroughly rinsed in clean water, and all the tape used to

Chris is seen here using a dashboard to ensure that a length of film is cut to the required length.

The film is then very, very carefully floated on to the surface of the warm water tank to ensure no bubbles are trapped under the film.

Once the film is on the surface of the water a chemical activator is sprayed on.

The part, or parts, are then gently rolled into the film, which attaches itself.

cover various holes removed; the parts are then left to air dry for ten to fifteen minutes.

Although the surface coating is durable and virtually resistant to damage at this stage, Wicked Coatings insist that every such coating receives a protective lacquer film before it leaves their workshops. I chose a gloss finish as I will be re-finishing the Ford dashboard with a two-part varnish before it goes back into the car.

In conclusion, water transfer printing or whatever you'd like to call it, is such a simple yet effective process that it's surely set to revolutionize the way coatings are applied to surfaces in the future.

Here we see an inner windscreen surround being lowered into the film.

The dashboard from a 1936 Ford being lifted out of the tank complete with its new burl walnut coating.

The centre facia panel and the glove-box lid from the 1936 Ford dashboard are see here being lifted from the tank.

After removal from the water tank the coated parts are thoroughly rinsed and left to air dry.

The newly coated dashboard receives a protecting coat of varnish before it leaves the workshop.

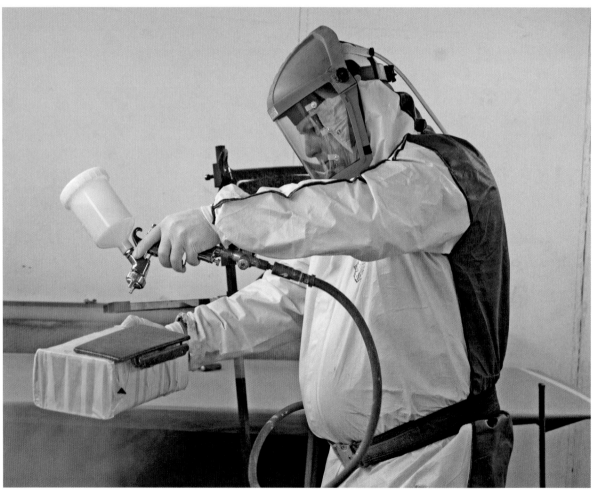

Smaller parts are taped to boxes to ensure they can be handled during the varnish spraying process.

This close-up of the burl walnut effect created by water transfer printing shows how realistic the results can be.

A 1930s Austin dashboard that was woodgrained using the Wicked Coatings process.

Sourcing Hardware

One of the most often overlooked aspects of any restoration or newbuild project is sourcing original specification hardware. Specialist suppliers of period handles, locks, hinges, window winders and the like do exist, but are few and far between. So one of the key messages is, try to ensure you collect as much of the original hardware as you can when you collect that project vehicle, even if they are only good for patterns.

I've previously mentioned the need almost to turn detective when pulling that wreck from a barn, the undergrowth or a farmer's field, and to cover the ground where it has lain with a metal detector, or even search on your hands and knees if needs be. While

Sourcing original-style hardware for any restoration project is not going to be easy.

some hardware can be sourced from specialists, other parts, particularly those that are unique to the wood-framed model in the product range, just won't be available as repros and you may end up scouring the country and paying an extortionate price for some obscure bracket or lock.

In general, many of the wood-framed vehicles built in-house by major manufacturers, and sold as their own products, are supported by car clubs and specialist suppliers today, as these usually carry a wide range of hardware fittings. However, vehicles supplied as a chassis/scuttle to a specialist body-builder usually ended up with hardware sourced from local suppliers, and trying to find a match today won't be

Barn finds can often be missing many hard-to-find and unique hardware, so check to see if everything is there.

an easy task. In some cases you may find suitable replacement fittings in unlikely places, such as the local boatyard or mobile home suppliers, and you may even find that parts from another vehicle type may be a good fit and match; in some extreme cases you may have to resort to getting parts custom made.

Trying to replicate a complicated corner bracket like this could be a slow, painful and costly exercise.

Dovetails that help locate a wooden door in perfect alignment are available for most US-built cars, but not every supplier carries those that are unique to the wooden-bodied station wagons. It pays to measure the old parts and to try and cross-reference them to repro parts if OEM part numbers don't match up with suppliers.

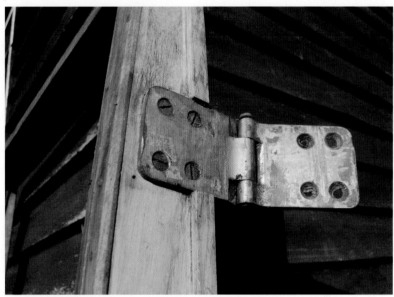

Heavy-duty brass hinges were used extensively in the coachbuilding trade. Replacements can be found at a few specialist suppliers.

In most cases the hinges available at your local hardware store just work on a vehicle. They won't be made strong enough to stand the wear and tear they will get on a vehicle, and the quality of metal used won't take the punishment of harsh weather conditions. On the other hand, heavy duty hinges can be sourced from specialists, but you may have to cut them to length, as seen in this trial fitting.

Even rusty brackets can be sand-blasted or used as templates for new parts, but trying to make such parts with no template could be time-consuming.

Piano hinges are popular for fitting tailgates, but it is essential to source a heavy duty steel version from a specialist. Aluminium or brass versions available at hardware stores are for household furniture only.

If mounting tailgate hardware in a non-original position it is essential to ensure that the upper tailgate can be raised high enough to avoid contact with your head when it is raised.

Tailgate hardware is available from specialist suppliers. The tailgate on my 1936 Ford uses a combination of reproduction swing-arm brackets from C & G in conjunction with notched lift arms sourced from a marine parts store.

LEFT: Some of the hardest-to-find hardware for wooden-bodied vehicles is that associated with opening windows. Many vehicles were built either without opening windows, or with fairly rudimentary glazing, because of the complications in designing opening windows in basic wooden frames.

BELOW: Many wood-framed vehicles were built with fairly basic window-opening mechanisms. However, those from other period vehicles can be re-engineered to fit, and give the driver the benefit of fully opening windows.

Sometimes it's easier to cut the inner panel containing locks and window winder mechanisms from an old period steel door. This can then be trimmed to fit the contours and shape of the wooden door.

Sliding side windows were a popular method of overcoming the problems of installing winding mechanisms. Here we see a version that has used the stainless-steel grab handles from a Morris Minor Traveller.

Sliding side-window grab handles from a Morris Minor Traveller come complete with locks.

Alternatively you can get an engineering shop to fold aluminium strip to the correct height of your windows.

I had these aluminium sliding window handles made up very cheaply. The small piece in the middle shows the cross-section that was a perfect fit for the edge of the glass.

Anybody who has travelled in the back of a convertible at any speed above 20mph will know what a cold and windswept experience it can be. Mike Gilroy found this adjustable rear screen at a parts meet and re-engineered it to fit his boat-tail convertible.

Adapting hardware, such as the door top mounted handles, to improve the aesthetics of the bodywork can require skilful engineering, but the result will be worth it.

Once seen on every street and highway, wooden truck bodies have now virtually disappeared into the history books, so hinges, latches and general ironwork may require the services of a blacksmith, if you can find one.

Suppliers and Resources

COACHBUILDERS, WOODWORKERS AND RESTORERS (USA)

Bodys by Boyd –
   contact Jeff Boyd
40140 Enterprise Dr
Oakhurst
CA 93644
Tel: (559) 683 7382
Email: bodysbyboyd@sti.net

Cincinnati Woodworks –
   contact Chip Kussmal
1974 Central Avenue
Cincinnati
OH 45214
Tel: (513) 721 8221
Email: cintiwood2@fuse.net

Heidens Woodworking –
   contact Ron Heiden
607 N.Vulcan
Leucadia
CA 92024
www.heidenswoodworking.com
Tel: (760) 753 8047
Email: tikibajabuig@hotmail.com

Redding Woodworks –
   contact Glenn Redding
6470 NW 90th Avenue
Ocala
FL 34482
Tel: (352) 351 5798
Email: arroyoni@yahoo.com

Rick Mack Enterprises –
   contact Rick Mack
PO Box 39631
Tacoma
WA 98439
www.rickmack.com
Tel: (253) 539 0432
Email: rjmccloskey@earthlink.net

Treehouse Woods –
   contact Erik Johnson
112 N. Brevard Avenue
Cocoa Beach
FL 32931
Tel: (321) 783 6781
Email: treehousewoods@earthlink.net

Wood N'Carr –
   contact Jeff and Suzy Carr
2345 Walnut Avenue
Signal Hill
CA 90755
Tel: (562) 498 8730
Email: SuzyQ22222@aol.com

COACHBUILDERS, WOODWORKERS AND RESTORERS (UK)

Clanfield Coachbuilding –
   contact Peter Bayliss
Unit E, Old Mill Lane
Little Clanfield
Clanfield
Bampton
OX18 2RX
www.coachbuilding.com
Tel: 01367 810326
Email: peter.baylis@btinternet.com

Classic Restorations Ltd –
   contact Warren Kennedy
Hulcote Farm
Salford Road
Hulcote
Milton Keynes
MK17 8BS
www.classicrestorations.org.uk
Tel: 01525 288481

Historic Vehicle Restoration
Unit 5 Trackside
Abbot Close
Byfleet
Surry KT14 7JN
Tel: 01932 347097
Email: sebmarshall@hotmail.co.uk

Rustytrucks Vintage Restoration Services
Woodbine Cottage
Warcop
Appleby in Westmorland
Cumbria
CA16 6PL
Tel: 01768 342656
Email: rustytrucks@mail2world.com

TDC Commercial Restorations
Watts Industrial Estate
Church Road
Lydney
Gloucestershire GL15 5EN
Tel: 01594 847135

Woodies –
    contact Steve Foreman
Unit 25 Eastmead Ind Estate
Lavant
Chichester
West Sussex PO18 0DB
www.morriswoodwork.co.uk
Tel: +44 01243 788660
Email: forwoodies@aol.com

WOODGRAINING RESOURCES

Grain-It Technologies Inc –
    contact Evan Westlake
334 Commerce Court
Winter Haven
FL 33880, USA
Tel: (863) 299 4494
Email: evan@woodgraining.com

Mac Pinstriping/Woodgraining
904 Winston
Houston
TX 77009
Tel: (713) 303 0883
www.macpinstriping.com

Wicked Coatings
44 Holton Road
Holton Heath Trading Park
Poole
Dorset BH16 6LT, UK
Tel: 01202 622258
www.wickedcoatings.co.uk
email: info@wickedcoatings.co.uk

HARDWARE RESOURCES

C & G Early Ford Parts Inc –
    (lots of Ford woodie hardware)
1941 Commercial Street
Escondido
CA 92029-1233, USA
www.cgfordparts.com
Tel: (760) 740 2400 or 800 266 0470
Email: info@cgfordparts.com

CLUBS AND ASSOCIATIONS

Woodie Car Club (UK)
www.woodiecarclub.com
Email: Woodguru@hotmail.co.uk

National Woodie Club (USA)
PO Box 6134
Lincoln
NE 68506, USA
www.nationalwoodieclub.com
Email: johnlee@nebrr.com

Index

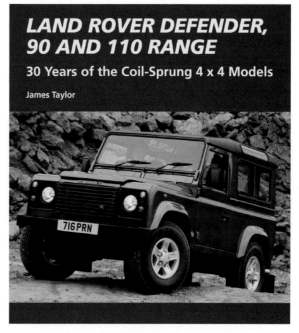
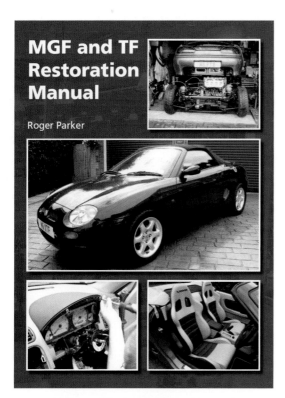
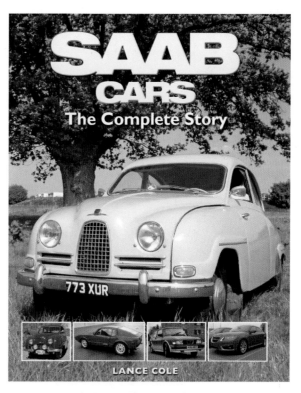